CAMBRIDGE MUSIC HANDBOOKS

Bach: The Brandenburg Concertos

CAMBRIDGE MUSIC HANDBOOKS

GENERAL EDITOR Julian Rushton

Cambridge Music Handbooks provide accessible introductions to major musical works, written by the most informed commentators in the field.

With the concert-goer, performer and student in mind, the books present essential information on the historical and musical context, the composition, and the performance and reception history of each work, or group of works, as well as critical discussion of the music.

Other published titles

Bach: Mass in B Minor JOHN BUTT
Beethoven: *Missa solemnis* WILLIAM DRABKIN
Beethoven: *Pastoral Symphony* DAVID WYN JONES
Beethoven: Symphony No 9 NICHOLAS COOK
Berg: Violin Concerto ANTHONY POPLE
Berlioz: *Roméo et Juliette* JULIAN RUSHTON
Chopin: The Four Ballades JIM SAMSON
Debussy: *La mer* SIMON TREZISE
Handel: *Messiah* DONALD BURROWS
Haydn: *The Creation* NICHOLAS TEMPERLEY
Haydn: String Quartets Op. 50 W. DEAN SUTCLIFFE
Holst: *The Planets* RICHARD GREENE
Janáček: *Glagolitic Mass* PAUL WINGFIELD
Mahler: Symphony No 3 PETER FRANKLIN
Mendelssohn: *The Hebrides* and other overtures R. LARRY TODD
Mozart: The 'Jupiter' Symphony ELAINE R. SISMAN
Musorgsky: *Pictures at an Exhibition* MICHAEL RUSS
Schoenberg: *Pierrot lunaire* JONATHAN DUNSBY
Schubert: *Die schöne Müllerin* SUSAN YOUENS
Schumann: Fantasie, Op. 17 NICHOLAS MARSTON
Sibelius: Symphony No 5 JAMES HEPOKOSKI
Strauss: *Also sprach Zarathustra* JOHN WILLIAMSON
Stravinsky: *Oedipus rex* STEPHEN WALSH
Verdi: Requiem DAVID ROSEN

Bach: The Brandenburg Concertos

Malcolm Boyd

PUBLISHED BY THE PRESS SYNDICATE OF THE UNIVERSITY OF CAMBRIDGE
The Pitt Building, Trumpington Street, Cambridge, United Kingdom

CAMBRIDGE UNIVERSITY PRESS
The Edinburgh Building, Cambridge CB2 2RU, UK   http://www.cup.cam.ac.uk
40 West 20th Street, New York, NY 10011–4211, USA   http://www.cup.org
10 Stamford Road, Oakleigh, Melbourne 3166, Australia
Ruiz de Alarcón 13, 28014 Madrid, Spain

© Cambridge University Press 1993

First published 1993
Reprinted 1995, 1997, 2000

Printed in the United Kingdom at the University Press, Cambridge

A catalogue record for this book is available from the British Library

Library of Congress Cataloguing in Publication data
Boyd, Malcolm.
Bach, the Brandenburg concertos / Malcolm Boyd.
p.   cm. – (Cambridge music handbooks)
Includes bibliographical references and index.
ISBN 0 521 38276 9 (hardback)–ISBN 0 521 38713 2 (paperback)
1. Bach, Johann Sebastian, 1685–1750. Brandenburgische Konzerte.
I. Title. II. Series.
ML410.B13B6   1993
784.2′4′092–dc20   92–39751 CIP MN

ISBN 0 521 38276 9 hardback
ISBN 0 521 38713 2 paperback

PE

Contents

Illustrations

*These pages are reproduced by kind permission of the
libraries concerned*

Preface

If the gramophone record catalogues are anything to go by, the Brandenburg Concertos enjoy a measure of popularity in Great Britain today which no other work by Bach and few by other composers can equal, and I suspect that the situation is similar in many other countries. The gramophone itself has undoubtedly contributed to this popularity, since most of the concertos do not easily lend themselves to concert performance by traditional orchestras and ensembles. The 'early music movement' has played its part, too, by allowing us to appreciate the variety of sonorities that Bach secured from his 'plusieurs instruments'. But more than anything else, it is the quality of the music itself that elicits such a wide response, not only among Bach enthusiasts and connoisseurs but also among unsophisticated listeners for whom much of Bach's other music can seem too complex and cerebral. Even more than the four orchestral suites, the Brandenburg Concertos show us the composer at his most cheerful and invigorating, and they are blessed with a tunefulness and rhythmic vitality which he rarely surpassed.

This is not to say that they pose no problems for the student and scholar (let alone the performer). Like every other major work by Bach, it seems, they raise questions which are difficult, and in some cases impossible, to answer – questions in response to which one can only offer, at best, plausible conjectures. In the present volume I have felt it part of my task to raise some of the more important textual and contextual problems that the sources present, even when I can offer no solutions to them. Not surprisingly, I am not the first to have devoted a short book to these marvellous works. J. A. Fuller-Maitland's little 'Musical Pilgrim' volume (1929) served a useful purpose in bringing the attention of English readers to what he took as 'experiments in the development of what was called the "concerto grosso"', while Norman Carrell's book (1963) is particularly valuable for its information on the instruments that

Bach composed for. Neither of these writers concerned himself much with evaluation of the sources. In Germany, Rudolf Gerber's slim but much-cited study of 1951 has been supplemented (and to a large extent superseded) by Elke Lang-Becker's *Bach: die Brandenburgischen Konzerte* (1990), which offers a detailed and perceptive structural analysis of each movement, as well as an informative chapter on 'Rezeptionsgeschichte' to which the present writer is indebted. Some of the most interesting and valuable results of recent research on the Brandenburg Concertos have appeared in periodicals, yearbooks or *Festschriften*, and these are listed in the Select Bibliography. By far the most important study of these works, however, is Michael Marissen's 'Scoring, Structure, and Signification in J. S. Bach's Brandenburg Concertos'. This meticulously researched and excellently written piece of work, completed as a PhD dissertation in 1991, did not come my way until the text of the present book was complete and ready for the press. I have not therefore been able to evaluate the sometimes controversial socio-political inferences that Marissen draws from the instrumentation and structure of the concertos, but I have drawn attention in the notes to some of the more important contexts in which his findings conflict with my own or reinforce them with new observations and insights.

Research for the present volume was facilitated by a travel grant from the Music Department of the University of Wales College of Cardiff and by the cooperation of the library staff there and at the Staatsbibliothek Preußischer Kulturbesitz, Berlin (in particular its director, Dr Helmut Hell). Dorothea Schröder was helpful in tracing various German writings, and I am grateful, too, to Julian Rushton and David Humphreys for helpful suggestions, and to David Wyn Jones for his careful proof-reading. As always, my wife Beryl lent encouragement, as well as ready advice on the niceties of the English language.

A note on editions

All the complete scores of the Brandenburg Concertos currently available in print present a text reliable enough for most purposes. The Bach-Gesellschaft (*BG*) edition of Wilhelm Rust (*Jahrgang* 19, 1869; Preface dated 1871) was based on the score that Bach wrote out for the Margrave of Brandenburg in 1721; it was reprinted as a miniature score in two volumes by Edwin F. Kalmus in 1968 (those who use it in conjunction with the present volume will need to insert bar numbers). It also served

Arnold Schering for the study scores he prepared for Eulenburg in 1927–9; these were revised with forewords by Roger Fiske in 1976. Kurt Soldan returned to the autograph score as the basis for his edition published by Peters-Verlag (and still available), which included a realization of the continuo bass by Ludwig Landshoff. A continuo realization, by Hans Gál, was also included in the edition made by Alfred Orel (Concerto No. 1) and Karl Geiringer (Nos. 2–6) for the Austrian Philharmonische Verlag (1939), but not in the pocket scores published two years later by Boosey and Hawkes.

In conformity with the editorial policy of the *Neue Bach-Ausgabe* (*NBA*), Heinrich Besseler consulted all available sources for his scholarly edition of 1956 (*NBA*, vol. VII/ii), which included, as an appendix, the early version of the first concerto (Alfred Dürr's edition of the early version of the fifth appeared as a supplement to this in 1975). The study score published in 1957 by Bärenreiter, and in East Germany by the Deutscher Verlag für Musik, reproduces Besseler's edition in smaller type. It ought to represent a 'best buy' for the modern student, especially as it prints each instrumental part at sounding pitch, but it falls short of the highest standards of editorial control and is marginally less accurate, as far as the actual notes are concerned, than either the *BG* edition or the more recent full scores edited by Werner Felix, Winnfried Hoffmann and Armin Schneiderheinze, which are issued separately by Breitkopf & Härtel (1985). These are not, however, available in small format.

For those with a more specialized interest in the text of the concertos, the facsimile edition of the dedication score published in 1950 by Peters, with a *Nachwort* by Peter Wackernagel, makes for fascinating study. It has long been out of print, however, and second-hand copies are now difficult to find.

As this book was going to press it was learnt that the two Berlin libraries mentioned therein, the Staatsbibliothek Preußische Kulturbesitz and the Deutsche Staatsbibliothek, had been reunited to form the Staatsbibliothek zu Berlin – Preußische Kulturbesitz.

Abbreviations

BD	*Bach-Dokumente*, ed. W. Neumann and H.-J. Schulze (Leipzig, 1963–72): vol. 1, *Schriftstücke von der Hand Johann Sebastian Bachs*; vol. 2, *Fremdschriftliche und gedruckte Dokumente zur Lebensgeschichte Johann Sebastian Bachs 1685–1750*; vol. 3, *Dokumente zum Nachwirken Johann Sebastian Bachs 1750–1800*
BG	*J. S. Bach: Werke* (the collected edition of Bach's works published by the Bach-Gesellschaft, Leipzig, 1851–99)
BWV	W. Schmieder, *Thematisch-systematisches Verzeichnis der musikalischen Werke Johann Sebastian Bachs: Bach-Werke-Verzeichnis* (Leipzig, 1950; 3rd edn, 1966)
HWV	B. Baselt, *Thematisch-systematische Verzeichnis (Händel-Handbuch)*, vols. 1–3 (Leipzig, 1978–86)
NBA	*Neue Bach-Ausgabe* (the collected edition of Bach's works published by the Johann-Sebastian-Bach Institut, Göttingen, and the Bach-Archiv, Leipzig (Kassel, 1954–))
RV	P. Ryom, *Répertoire des Œuvres d'Antonio Vivaldi: les compositions instrumentales* (Copenhagen, 1986)

Pitch notation

In the text specific pitches are indicated by reference to the Helmholtz system, in which middle C is shown as c', the octaves above as c'' and c''' and those below as c and C (always in italics); the changeover from one octave to the next is reckoned from the note C, and not from A.

1

Background

The concerto was to the late Baroque what the symphony was to the Classical era: the most popular and important genre of instrumental music. Only the orchestral suite, outside vocal music, brought together as many musicians at one time, and the concerto had an advantage over the suite in that it provided greater opportunity for virtuoso display, so that a patron or prince might take delight not only in the size but also in the technical capabilities of the orchestra at his disposal. The concerto was also a particularly versatile genre when it came to the forces necessary to perform it. A concerto grosso of the type written by Corelli, for instance, might be played by as few as three or four musicians, simply by dispensing with the *ripieno* (or tutti) parts, or by as many as sixty or more with the *ripieno* parts doubled many times over, perhaps by woodwind and brass instruments as well as by strings.[1] Once the concerto became established in Italy during the last decades of the seventeenth century, there were few composers in the major European centres who were not drawn to its various possibilities, and few orchestras and music societies that did not avail themselves of the ever-increasing repertory of such works at their disposal.

In the concertos of Arcangelo Corelli (1653–1713) and his imitators the virtuoso element was to some extent constrained by the texture of the music, an expansion of the contrapuntal trio sonata. This was perfectly in tune with the conservative taste that held sway in Rome, but it was soon to be rendered old-fashioned (though not completely outmoded) by the newer type of solo concerto, in the formation of which Corelli's contemporary Giuseppe Torelli (1658–1709) played an important part. Like Corelli, Torelli had been trained in Bologna and, taking his cue from the brilliant sonatas for trumpet that he and others wrote for performance in the basilica of San Petronio, he began to cultivate there a newer type of concerto that placed a single soloist (usually a violinist) in the limelight.

Torelli spent about two years (1697–9) in Ansbach as *maestro di concerto* to Margrave Georg Friedrich of Brandenburg-Ansbach, a distant cousin of the margrave to whom Bach later dedicated his concertos.[2] Relations between Ansbach and the Berlin court were close, and in 1697 the Electress Sophie Charlotte 'borrowed' both Torelli and the margrave's *Kapellmeister*, F. A. M. Pistocchi (1659–1726), for her own music-making in Berlin. The following year Torelli dedicated his twelve *Concerti musicali* Op. 6 (1698) to the electress, and the Berlin court's particular association with the concerto might well date from this time.

Tomaso Albinoni (1671–1751) and Antonio Vivaldi (1678–1741) were Torelli's principal successors in developing the newer type of concerto that was to exist alongside the Corellian concerto grosso and eventually to supplant it. Both composers were born, died and spent most of their working lives in Venice, and the type of concerto they established, in three movements and with the ritornello structure favoured for the outer movements, has sometimes been called the 'Venetian concerto', though it was soon taken up throughout Europe. That Vivaldi left more than 450 concertos and Albinoni only about 60 is less important than the fact that most of their contemporaries would have regarded them principally as opera composers (a genre in which their achievements are numerically more or less equal). Connexions between the da capo aria and the concerto's ritornello structure (which assume special importance in Bach's work) will be explored later, but it cannot be without some significance that Corelli is not known to have composed operas or very much in other vocal genres.[3]

The concerto seems to have claimed Bach's attention during three quite distinct periods of his life and in three quite different ways. The first period, at Weimar in 1713–14, might be described as one of apprenticeship. As court organist and chamber musician (and from 2 March 1714 *Konzertmeister*) to Duke Wilhelm Ernst, Bach came into close contact with the young Prince Johann Ernst (1696–1715), the duke's nephew and an enthusiastic admirer of Italian music, especially Italian concertos. He evidently brought back both printed and manuscript copies from the Netherlands, where he had studied for two years at the University of Utrecht, and he also composed Italianate concertos himself, some of which were published by Telemann in 1718, three years after the prince's death at the early age of nineteen. But it seems that Johann Ernst's appetite for concertos was not easily satisfied, and he evidently got his teacher J. G. Walther, a kinsman of Bach's, and Bach himself to arrange such works for solo organ or harpsichord. Fourteen of Walther's arrangements and some twenty of Bach's remain. Bach's contributions to this enterprise include four works by the prince himself and one by Telemann, but it is the modern Venetians, and especially Vivaldi, who are most strongly represented, and it is to them that we must look for the roots of Bach's concerto style.

The reputation that Weimar achieved at this time as a centre for Italian music, and particularly Italian concertos, is reflected in a petition which the young Augsburg musician Philipp David Kräuter (1690–1741) addressed to his ecclesiastical employers in 1713. Kräuter had gone to Weimar the previous year and studied there with Bach. On 10 April 1713 he requested an extension of his leave from Augsburg in order

firstly to complete my studies in both composition and the playing of keyboard and other instruments, and with God's help to make greater strides in my art; and, secondly, because the prince of the Weimar court [Johann Ernst], who is not only an excellent musical dilettante but also an incomparable violinist, will return to Weimar from Holland after Easter and remain there during the summer, and so it will be possible for me to hear a good deal of fine Italian and French music, from which I will benefit in composing concertos and overtures . . .[4]

But it was not only through Johann Ernst and the Weimar court that Bach came into contact with Vivaldi's music and the new concerto styles at this time. As mentioned earlier, Torelli's presence in 1697–9 had brought the late seventeenth-century Italian concerto style to Ansbach, and through the court there to Berlin. The German violinist Johann Georg Pisendel (1687–1755) was also at Ansbach, where he studied with Torelli and later played in the court orchestra. In 1709 he went to Leipzig, and on the way he broke his journey to visit Bach at Weimar, no doubt bringing with him some Italian concertos, including the violin concerto by Albinoni that he was to perform with the collegium musicum at Leipzig. Founded in 1702 by Telemann, the collegium musicum was directed at the time by Melchior Hoffmann (c.1685–1715), who increased its membership to about forty musicians. In 1712 Pisendel obtained employment in the Dresden court orchestra and in 1716–17 he visited Italy, where he studied with Vivaldi in Venice and established a firm friendship with him, as a result of which Vivaldi wrote several concertos expressly for Pisendel and the Dresden court orchestra. Bach's connexions with Dresden date at the latest from 1717, the year of his famous 'duel' with the French harpsichordist and organist Louis Marchand, which was decided in Bach's favour when Marchand withdrew from the scene of battle without a note being struck.

Bach had numerous opportunities, then, to familiarize himself with Italian concertos before he left Weimar in December 1717, and the effect of this was soon to be observed, for example in the structure and figuration of the sonata that introduces the Easter Cantata, No. 31, *Der Himmel lacht* (1715). Bach's own first essays in concerto writing may possibly date from the Weimar years, but it was probably not until he was appointed *Kapellmeister* to Prince Leopold of Anhalt-Cöthen in 1717 that he was able to devote himself to the composition of concertos in any systematic way. Prince Leopold was a keen musician and by 1713, when he returned to Cöthen after a period of study in Berlin and a tour of the Low Countries, England, France and Italy, he was a competent performer on the violin, bass viol and harpsichord. He soon set about creating what he called his 'collegium musicum', a permanent and fully professional court *Kapelle* which by 1716, when the prince attained his majority and succeeded his late father as ruler, consisted of seventeen musicians, including the *Kapellmeister*, Augustin Reinhard Stricker. Seven of these had been recruited from Berlin when the new Prussian king, Friedrich Wilhelm I, disbanded his orchestra there in 1713.

When Bach succeeded Stricker as *Kapellmeister* in 1717 the constitution of the collegium musicum was as follows:

Joseph Spiess, violin	Johann Ludwig Schreiber, trumpet
Martin Friedrich Marcus, violin	
Emanuel Heinrich Gottlieb Freytag, violin	Johann Christoph Krahl, trumpet
Christian Ferdinand Abel, bass viol	Anton Unger, timpani
Christian Bernhard Linigke, cello	Johann Christian Kreyser, organ
Johann Heinrich Freytag, flute	
Johann Gottlieb Würdig, flute	Johann Freytag, 'ripienista'
Johann Ludwig Rose, oboe	Wilhelm Andreas Harbordt, 'ripienista'
Johann Christoph Torlée, bassoon	Adam Ludwig Weber, 'ripienista'.

The last three musicians on this list were evidently employed as 'rank-and-file' instrumentalists, required only for doubling parts; each is entered in the payment lists as 'Musicus', as distinct from the more elevated title of 'Cammer-Musicus' enjoyed by the better-paid members of the collegium musicum.[5] Assuming the participation of Prince Leopold on the bass viol and of Bach himself (perhaps as viola player, if not at the harpsichord), we have here the forces required for most, if not all, of the six Brandenburg Concertos. The third concerto would seem to demand two viola players and two cellists in addition to those available from the collegium musicum; and, unless the trumpeters were able to double on horns (which is perhaps unlikely given the highly specialized technique called for on both instruments), the Cöthen band would have needed the services of extra players for the First Brandenburg Concerto. Supplementary players were in fact employed a number of times, and the presence at court of two horn players on 6 June 1722 might well have been one occasion for a performance of that work.

It is reasonable to assume that the Brandenburg Concertos were played by, and for the most part composed for, the orchestra at Cöthen. How many other concertos Bach wrote for the same players we do not know. Supposition takes the place of hard evidence in assigning the two solo violin concertos (BWV 1041-2) and the Concerto in D minor for two violins (BWV 1043) to the Cöthen years: autograph material exists only for the A minor and D minor concertos (and then only in part), and all these concertos (including the Brandenburgs) were unknown to Bach's first biographer, Johann Nicolaus Forkel. Bach's predilection for composing in a particular genre more or less systematically over a period of time, returning to it only to bring a corpus of works to their final form, reinforces the theory that it was at Cöthen that the composer wrote his original concertos, that these numbered many more than the nine that are known to us, and that some of them are to be found in transcriptions for one or more harpsichords and strings that Bach made during his time at Leipzig.[6]

It was in Spring 1729 that Bach first accepted control of the collegium musicum that Telemann had founded in Leipzig in 1702. The term 'collegium musicum' is not used in this connexion in the same way that Prince Leopold used it at Cöthen – for a regularly constituted professional ensemble – but rather in its more usual sense of a music society at which students, amateurs and perhaps semi-professionals met regularly to make music for their own enjoyment and that of anyone who cared to listen. Bach's society met weekly at Gottfried Zimmermann's coffee house in the Catherinenstraße, or during the summer months at the same Zimmermann's garden outside the city. Its members were frequently called upon to provide music on special civic or academic occasions elsewhere in the city, but it would be for the ordinary weekly meetings that Bach made his concerto transcriptions. They include versions for harpsichord(s) and strings of the violin concertos BWV 1041–3 and the Fourth Brandenburg Concerto, as well as Vivaldi's A minor Concerto for four violins (RV 580) and other concertos by Bach of which the original versions have been lost. It may be assumed that in the concertos for more than one harpsichord Bach would have been joined as soloist by his eldest sons, but although he continued to direct the collegium musicum at least until 1741 (with a break of two years between 1737 and 1739) the activity does not seem to have stimulated him to compose entirely new concertos. None, at least, is known to date from this period. As far as original composition is concerned, he seems to have exhausted his interest in the genre at Cöthen, or at least in the early Leipzig years.

Bach's historical position at the culmination of an era, manning one of the last bastions of the Baroque in the face of an encroaching *galant* style in music, has tended to obscure the fact that very little in the way of a native tradition stands behind the Brandenburg Concertos. It is true, of course, that the concerto as a genre was about forty years old by the time the Brandenburgs were composed; Georg Muffat (1653–1704) had heard concertos by Corelli in Rome in the early 1680s and claimed credit for introducing the genre to Germany on his return in 1682. But the concertos that Muffat himself composed and published in Salzburg and Passau were, quite naturally, of the conservative Roman type and much influenced by the French orchestral suite (Muffat had studied with Lully in Paris), as were the concertos and concerto-like works of other south German composers such as Benedict Anton Aufschnaiter (1665–1742) and Johann Christoph Pez (1664–1716). Johann Sigismund Kusser (1660–1727), another pupil of Lully, and Georg Philipp Telemann (1681–1767) were among other composers who preferred the French-influenced orchestral suite to the concerto. The more modern style of the Venetian concerto made rapid inroads, especially in more northerly parts, when it eventually reached Germany, and Bach was not the only German composer whose music was affected by it. As Pippa Drummond has written,

the main impact of the new form was felt in the second decade of the [eighteenth] century. It is at this stage that references to Vivaldi's concertos begin to appear in German literature and correspondence; at this stage, too, that a whole generation of young composers (Stölzel, Heinichen, and Pisendel, to name but a few) sought tuition from Italy's leading concertists.[7]

It is highly likely that by 1721 Bach was familiar with concertos by each of the three German composers mentioned by Drummond, but in the absence of a firm chronology for any of them it is impossible to suggest how many and which concertos Bach might have known. He would certainly have known some by Telemann, with whom he was on friendly terms from about 1706, but whether these would have been of the Venetian type or of Telemann's preferred Roman type one cannot say. Joseph Meck (1690–1758), who worked at the Eichstätt court as violinist from 1711 and became *Hofkapellmeister* there in 1721, is another composer whose concertos Bach would certainly have been acquainted with. Meck is credited with being the first German to publish a set of solo concertos.[8] They appeared in 1720–21, at the same time that Bach was working on the Brandenburg Concertos and, like the Meck concerto that J. G. Walther arranged for organ, they are all in the Vivaldian three-movement form.

It seems certain, though, that Bach's familiarity with the Venetian concerto style came directly from hearing and studying Italian examples, especially those of Vivaldi, rather than through the works of his German contemporaries. The fundamental importance of Vivaldi to the formation of Bach's concerto style was recognized by the latter's earliest biographer, who was undoubtedly informed on the subject by C. P. E. Bach, and through him by J. S. Bach himself. Forkel wrote:

John Sebastian Bach's first attempts at composition were, like all first attempts, defective.... He soon began to feel that the eternal running and leaping led to nothing; that there must be order, connection, and proportion in the thoughts; and that, to attain such objects, some kind of guide was necessary. Vivaldi's Concertos for the violin, which were then just published, served him for such a guide. He so often heard them praised as admirable compositions, that he conceived the happy idea of arranging them all for his clavichord. He studied the chain of the ideas, their relation to each other, the variations of the modulations, and many other particulars. The change necessary to be made in the ideas and passages, composed for the violin, but not suitable to the clavichord, taught him to think musically ...[9]

and later:

[Bach's] ardent genius was attended by an equally ardent industry, which incessantly impelled him, when he could not succeed by his own strength, to seek aid from the models existing in his time. At first, Vivaldi's violin concertos afforded him this assistance ...[10]

Modern Bach scholars, including Christoph Wolff, have on the whole confirmed Forkel's opinion of the over-riding importance of Vivaldi's influence:

Vivaldi's concertos ... confronted him [Bach] with an entirely new set of problems and possibilities. This is not to say that Vivaldi was the first and only one to develop a new compositional concept, but he certainly was the principal exponent of a new way of musical composition based on genuine 'musical thinking' exemplified first and foremost in his concertos ...[11]

Some idea of the nature and extent of Vivaldi's influence on the concertos of Bach will, I hope, become apparent from the pages that follow.[12]

2

Genesis and reception

Most of what we know about Margrave Christian Ludwig of Brandenburg we owe to the researches of Heinrich Besseler.[1] The dedicatee of Bach's Brandenburg Concertos was born on 14 May 1677 to the second wife of the Elector Friedrich Wilhelm of Brandenburg, whose far-reaching reforms laid the foundations for the kingdom of Prussia and earned him the name of the Great Elector. Friedrich Wilhelm died in 1688 and was succeeded by his son and heir (Christian Ludwig's half-brother), Friedrich, who reigned as elector from 1688 and as King Friedrich I of Prussia from 1701 until his death in 1713. The king was a cultured man and a generous patron; in 1696 he founded an Academy of Arts in Berlin, and four years later an Academy of Sciences headed by Leibnitz. In his leanings towards intellectual pursuits he was encouraged by his musically gifted wife, Sophie Charlotte, for whom he built the Schloss Charlottenburg, which became a glittering centre for music in the early years of the eighteenth century.

Things changed abruptly in Berlin when Friedrich Wilhelm I (the 'Soldier King') succeeded his father in 1713. One of his first acts as ruler was to dismiss all the musicians (some of whom found employment at Cöthen and were later Bach's colleagues there), but he allowed his uncle Christian Ludwig to remain in residence at the Berlin Schloss and to retain his own *Kapelle*; he also made over to him for life estates in Malchow and Heinersdorf, about five miles from the Schloss, which the margrave used as a summer residence. While the king led a philistine life, concentrating his energies on building up the military strength of his kingdom, Christian Ludwig seems to have done his best to maintain the cultural traditions of his late half-brother. He evidently had the means to do it: in 1734 his income amounted to the considerable sum of 48,945 Thalers. A good deal of this was presumably spent on the musical establishment, but we know the names of only six of his *Kammermusici*:

9

those who were paid twenty-five Thalers each for mourning dress at his funeral (he died on 3 September 1734). They appear in the account books as Emmerling, Kotowsky, Hagen, Kühltau, Emis and Ellinger. Cyriak Emmerling (*c*.1660–1737), listed in Walther's *Musicalisches Lexicon* as a composer, keyboard player and bass viol player born in Eisleben,[2] was evidently the margrave's *Kapellmeister*; Besseler identified Kotowsky as probably the father of the flautist Georg Wilhelm Kottowsky (born in 1735 according to Eitner)[3] and Kühltau as the bassoonist Samuel Kühltau, who in 1754 was a member of the royal *Kapelle* in Berlin and died soon afterwards.

It does not follow, however, that the six who were provided with mourning clothes were the only musicians in the margrave's household in 1734; neither should it be assumed that his *Kapelle* had remained at the same size as it was when Bach visited Berlin fifteen years earlier. The purpose of Bach's visit in 1719, for which the sum of 130 Thalers was made over to him from the Cöthen exchequer on 1 March, was to pay for a new harpsichord which had been ordered for Prince Leopold from the instrument-builder to the Berlin court, Michael Mietke. Besseler suggested that Bach must have made an earlier visit, some time after 15 June 1718, to place the order in person, but there is no documentary evidence for such a visit, and no compelling reason for supposing it to have taken place. The specification for the new instrument could perfectly well have been sent by post or messenger, but Bach's presence would have been necessary in 1719, not only to pay for the harpsichord but also to inspect it and to make arrangements for transporting it from Berlin. Possibly Bach himself travelled back with it to Cöthen, where it arrived on 14 March 1719.

It must have been this Berlin visit that Bach referred to in his dedication of the Brandenburg Concertos, dated 24 March 1721, when he spoke of playing before the margrave 'il y a une couple d'années' and receiving his request for 'quelques pieces de ma Composition'. Written in courtly French and in a conventionally obsequious style (made the more so in the original by the writer's consistent use of the third person in addressing the margrave), it reads:

> To His Royal Highness
> Monseigneur
> Crétien Louis
> Marggraf de Brandenbourg &c. &c. &c.
> Monseigneur

As I had the pleasure a couple of years ago of being heard by Your Royal Highness, in accordance with your commands, and of observing that you took some delight in the small musical talent that Heaven has granted me, and as, when I took my leave of Your Royal Highness, you did me the honour of requesting that I send you some of my compositions, I have therefore followed your most gracious commands and taken the liberty of discharging my humble obligation to Your Royal Highness with the present concertos which I have adapted to several instruments, begging you most humbly not to judge their imperfections by the standards of that refined and delicate taste in music that everyone knows you to possess, but rather to accept, with benign consideration, the profound respect and most humble devotion that I attempt to show by this means. For the rest, Monseigneur, I most humbly beg Your Royal Highness to be so kind as to continue your good grace towards me, and to be assured that I desire nothing more than to be employed on occasions more worthy of you and your service, being with unparalleled zeal,

      Monseigneur,

           Your Royal Highness's

                      most humble and most obedient servant,

Coethen, 24 March 1721   Jean Sebastien Bach

The score in Bach's hand that bears this dedication is the major source for the Brandenburg Concertos, but it is not the only one.[4] Others include copies of the first three concertos made by Christian Friedrich Penzel (1737–1801), who studied at the Thomasschule in Leipzig shortly after Bach's death and was for a short time in charge of the choir there. Penzel's copies of the score and parts of the First Concerto are particularly valuable because, although they were made some ten years after Bach's death, they transmit versions of the concerto that pre-date the autograph score of 1721. Sources also exist for an early version of the Fifth Concerto. Even without these, however, one might easily deduce that the Brandenburg Concertos did not originate with the margrave's commission but were composed over a period of years, probably beginning even before Bach's appointment in 1717 as *Kapellmeister* at Cöthen.

The story of their composition might well begin in 1713, during the period of Bach's employment as organist and chamber musician to Duke Wilhelm Ernst of Weimar. In February of that year Bach and other members of the Weimar *Kapelle* visited Weissenfels, where, in the imposing castle that overlooks the town, Duke Christian of Saxony-Weissenfels had reigned for a year. Given the close ties between the courts of Weimar and Weissenfels, this was probably not Bach's first visit, and it was certainly not his last. His second wife, Anna Magdalena Wilcke, whom he married in 1721, was the daughter of a court trumpeter at Weissenfels, and in 1729 Bach secured for himself the courtesy title of *Kapellmeister von Haus aus* to the Court of Saxony-Weissenfels. His visit in 1713 coincided with preparations for the birthday of Duke Christian on 23 February, and it was almost certainly for this occasion that the so-called Hunting Cantata, *Was mir behagt, ist nur die muntre Jagd* (BWV 208), was composed. This is in no fewer than fifteen sections, six of them recitatives and the rest lyrical movements (arias, choruses and one duet); the score calls for two recorders, three oboes (one of them a *taille*, or tenor oboe), two horns, bassoon, strings and continuo. What is unusual for a homage cantata of such dimensions is that, in the form in which it has come down to us, it begins neither with an imposing chorus nor with an instrumental introduction, but with a simple recitative accompanied by continuo only. Among Bach's other works, however, is one entitled 'Sinfonia', which Wolfgang Schmieder included in his Bach catalogue as BWV 1071. This is in the same key (F major) as the cantata and is scored for an identical ensemble, except that it does not require flutes.[5] Its particular relevance for us here is that it consists essentially of the first, second and last movements (minus the polonaise) of the First Brandenburg Concerto. It is, in fact, the copy by Penzel alluded to above.

The term 'sinfonia' is one that Bach and his contemporaries normally used for an introduction, or overture, to a longer work; and, as Johannes Krey first pointed out,[6] there are good reasons for supposing that BWV 1071 originally served to introduce BWV 208. Not only do the key and instrumentation match exactly,[7] but the opening horn phrases of the sinfonia (Ex. 1b) clearly suggest a hunting-call; Horace Fitzpatrick has, in fact, identified an early eighteenth-century 'Greeting Call' which resembles them very closely (Ex. 1a).[8] It might be worth mentioning also that the opening notes of the cantata itself echo the first notes of the sinfonia's violin theme (Ex. 1c).[9]

It seems unlikely, though, that the sinfonia served as an introduction to Cantata No. 208 in exactly the form in which it exists in Penzel's copy. In the first place, its dimensions far exceed those of other cantata sinfonias, which consist as a rule of a single movement only (Bach did, in fact, re-use the first movement alone as the sinfonia to Cantata No. 52 in 1726). Also, there are a number of places where Penzel's score differs from the Brandenburg version in ways which, as will be shown later (see

Ex. 1   (a) Early eighteenth-century Greeting Call

(b) Brandenburg Concerto No. 1, first movement

(c) Cantata No. 208/i

Was mir be-hagt,   ist   nur   die muntre Jagd!

p. 71), suggest the intervention of another hand. Perhaps only the first movement originated with the cantata, the other two being stages on the way to Brandenburg Concerto No. 1. Indeed, both Julien Tiersot and Rudolf Gerber were of the opinion that Penzel's copy represents a late arrangement of Brandenburg No. 1 – a transformation of a concerto-suite organism into the fast–slow–minuet format of the operatic and concert sinfonia in vogue from about the middle of the eighteenth century.[10]

The general suitability of the sinfonia's first movement to the 'Hunting Cantata' is, however, not the only reason for supposing this version of the work to be earlier than that in Bach's presentation copy. An examination of those passages in which the actual notes differ in the two versions (leaving aside differences that might result from the intervention of someone other than Bach himself) is inconclusive: in some cases the concerto version seems to be an improvement on the sinfonia, in others the reverse seems to apply. Errors in the violino piccolo part (notated in D), however, strongly suggest that the presentation score was copied from a version (such as Penzel's) which included a violin tuned at the normal pitch; at bar 22 in the first movement and bar 17 in the second a flat sign has been changed into a natural, while there are mistranscriptions a third too high at bar 8 (uncorrected) and bar 30 (corrected) in the first movement. Such errors must support the supposition that the violino piccolo was not included in Bach's original version of these movements

13

(or, presumably, of the minuet), but was added when the margrave's score was copied out.

While the sinfonia's connexion with Cantata No. 208 remains conjectural,[11] its identity as an early version of the First Brandenburg Concerto (or at least of three movements from that work) has been 'officially' acknowledged by a change of BWV number from 1071 to 1046*a*. Whether or not any other movements in the Brandenburgs pre-date this sinfonia is a question that has attracted much speculation. In 1956, before the evidence of Bach's visit to Weissenfels in 1713 had come to light, Heinrich Besseler proposed the following chronology:[12]

c.1718:   Concerto No. 6; Concerto No. 1, first version (BWV 1071); Concerto No. 3

c.1719:   Concerto No. 2; Concerto No. 1 (third movement); Concerto No. 4

c.1720:   Concerto No. 5.

Except for his very reasonable assumption that Bach tailored the concertos to the forces of Prince Leopold's collegium musicum at Cöthen, Besseler adduces little evidence to support his chronology, and his claim to recognize stylistic differences between works separated by only a year or two seems particularly over-ambitious.[13] Even bolder claims have been made for the dating of some of the concertos, however. The scoring of No. 6, with viols and violas but without violins, has led many commentators to place it earlier than all the other concertos; '?1708–10' is the date given for it in the *New Grove*,[14] and Thurston Dart argued that it might even have originated during Bach's period as organist of the Neuekirche at Arnstadt (1703–7).[15] It seems unlikely, though, that Bach would have composed a ritornello structure as fully developed as the first movement of Brandenburg Concerto No. 6, or as neat and conventional a da capo structure as the last movement of that work at a time when he was still employing only more antiquated structures for his cantata arias. The instrumentation might seem old-fashioned, but in fact it was well suited to the Cöthen band, and especially to a small group of players such as Prince Leopold might have taken with him on one of his visits to the spa at Carlsbad. (The prince himself, an able viol player, might indeed have been a member of the ensemble in the early performances.)

Martin Geck proposed a date of 1713 for this concerto and suggested that it was, at least in part, an arrangement of an earlier trio sonata; he also proposed 1713 as the *terminus ad quem* of No. 3, arguing that it may have originated as an introduction to a church cantata.[16] A Weissenfels origin for the Second Brandenburg Concerto has been suggested by Martin Bernstein, who argues that only there would Bach have found a virtuoso capable of playing the solo trumpet part (namely Johann Caspar Altenburg (1689–1761), who led the corps of trumpeters at the Weissenfels court and was known particularly for his playing in the high 'clarino' range).[17] The fact remains that the only thing that can be said with certainty about the chronology of the Brandenburg Concertos is that they were all composed by March 1721, the date on Bach's autograph copy. Beyond this lies the reasonable hypothesis that part of the first concerto served to introduce the 'Hunting Cantata' in 1713, or (more likely, perhaps) at a repeat performance some years later, and the plausible assumption that the fifth concerto was the last to be composed and that its composition was prompted by the purchase of the new harpsichord for the Cöthen *Kapelle* in 1719.

This last observation brings us back to Bach's visit to Berlin in February or March of that year. The beautiful and costly new instrument that he had been sent to examine and pay for was the work of Michael Mietke (*d.*1719), the court harpsichord builder at Schloss Charlottenburg. A splendid example of his work – a single-manual harpsichord japanned in white and decorated by the renowned Flemish furniture maker and decorator, Gerard Dagly – may be seen there today, and it may have been on this instrument, and probably others by Mietke as well, that Bach played to the margrave in 1719.[18] The Mietke that he took back with him to Cöthen, however, was a two-manual instrument, and its fine quality must have made it the centre of attraction in its new home. What more natural than that Bach should compose a new piece to show its paces – one which for the first time in history elevated the harpsichord from continuo instrument to a position of *primus inter pares* in the solo group of a concerto, with an imposing solo 'cadenza' to boot.

As already mentioned, it has been suggested that the Fifth Brandenburg Concerto was composed to fulfil this very function – to inaugurate the new harpsichord from Berlin – and in support of this it has been pointed out that, although the concerto is in D major, the highest note in the harpsichord part is $c\natural'''$, two octaves above middle C; this was also the highest note on the two Mietke harpsichords now in the Charlottenburg.[19] There exists, however, an earlier version of the concerto, a set of parts mainly in the hand of Bach's pupil and son-in-law Johann Christoph Altnikol, in which the compass of the solo harpsichord might point to the opposite conclusion. In this version the low B' at bar 92 in the first movement is notated an octave higher, obviously for an instrument which extended downwards only as far as C.[20] We seem, therefore, to be faced with two possibilities: either the instrument that Mietke built for the Cöthen court extended downwards only as far as C, but Bach adjusted bar 92 on the presentation score, knowing that the margrave's instruments were capable of reaching it; or the early version of the Fifth Brandenburg Concerto pre-dates the arrival of the new instrument in Cöthen. The main difference between the two versions lies in the 'cadenza', which in the 'Brandenburg' recension has been expanded from eighteen to sixty-five bars. Possibly it was with this new and unprecedentedly elaborate cadenza that Bach celebrated the arrival of the new instrument from Berlin.[21]

It has sometimes been argued that, with a large proportion of the six concertos already in existence by 1719, Bach took an unconscionably long time to complete the presentation score, and that this betokens a lack of interest on his part in fulfilling the margrave's commission. But, quite apart from the fact that we do not really know how many of the eighteen concerto movements were already written (almost certainly seven or eight and probably more, but with a good deal of rewriting still to be done), the twenty-four months separating the commission and its completion were troubled ones for Bach. In addition to his usual duties at Cöthen, there was at least one visit to Carlsbad with Prince Leopold and another to Halle, where he competed for (and in the end declined) the post of organist at the Jakobikirche; these months saw also the deaths of his son Leopold Augustus (aged ten months), his wife Maria Barbara and his brother Johann Christoph, the compilation of the *Clavier-Büchlein* for Wilhelm Friedemann Bach, the completion of the sonatas and suites for solo violin and the composition of a number of other works. In a letter written in October 1730 to his former schoolfriend Georg Erdmann, Bach spoke of the 'gracious prince [Leopold] who both loved and understood music, and with whom I had expected to end my days', but Bach's satisfaction with Cöthen (at least in retrospect) did not prevent his applying for the Halle post, and it is possible to interpret the dedication of the Brandenburg Concertos, and perhaps explain their relatively late delivery, as part of another attempt to change his station.

One other factor needs to be taken into account. Besseler argued, and all subsequent writers seem to have agreed with him, that when Bach came to compile the presentation copy of the Brandenburg Concertos for

Margrave Christian Ludwig he was able to select the six works from a much larger corpus of such compositions already to hand. Neither Besseler nor anyone else, however, has brought forward documentary proof of this, and what evidence there is might lead one to the opposite conclusion. In the first place, of Bach's extant concertos apart from the Brandenburgs only two, the Concerto in A minor for flute, violin and harpsichord (BWV 1044) and the putative original (for violin and oboe) of the Concerto in C minor for two harpsichords (BWV 1060), might have found an appropriate place in a set of concertos 'avec plusieurs instruments'; but BWV 1044, as a concerto, seems to date from the 1730s (although its constituent movements apparently existed earlier in different forms), and there is no proof, either, that BWV 1060 was in existence by March 1721. Are we to assume, then, that the storehouse of Brandenburg-type concertos existing in 1721 has been completely lost? Peter Williams has speculated on the possibility that the Sonata in G minor for bass viol and harpsichord, BWV 1029, may have originated as a concerto – possibly even one which Bach might have included in the Brandenburg set, had he chosen to do so.[22] Other works of this type were almost certainly adapted for use in cantatas, but there cannot be many of these.[23] In fact, the heterogeneous origins of Brandenburg Concerto No. 1, and possibly of No. 3 as well, might suggest that Bach experienced some difficulty in getting together six concertos 'avec plusieurs instruments', and this again could have been a reason for the delay in responding to the margrave's request.

One frequently finds the opinion expressed that the margrave made no use at all of the score Bach sent him, but merely added it to his library shelves and left it there. There are no grounds at all for thinking this. We should not take it that the six musicians paid for mourning dress in 1734 indicated the size of the margrave's *Kapelle* at that time, and we know nothing at all about its composition in 1719–21, but it seems unlikely that Bach would have sent him six concertos totally unsuitable for his musicians to play. Nor does the fact that no record exists of the margrave having rewarded Bach for his work (or even acknowledged it) mean that no acknowledgment was made. It is also mistaken to deduce from the clean state of the manuscript itself that no use was made of it, for the margrave would certainly have had the necessary parts copied and retained the original score for his library. It should also be noted that the special layout of the fifth concerto in this score was probably adopted to facilitate performance (see below, p. 39).

17

The inventory of the margrave's music library, drawn up in some haste after his death, is an important but tantalizing document: important because it reveals the extent of his musical sympathies, tantalizing because in many instances it lacks the detail we should like to have. Some fifty opera scores are included, the composers most prominently represented being Handel with seven such works, Francesco Conti with six and Giuseppe Maria Orlandini with four. Of particular interest in the present context is the large number of concertos included among the instrumental works: more than 250 in all, the composers mentioned being Albinoni, Brescianello, J. J. Kress, Locatelli, Mauro (perhaps Tommaso de Mauro), Valentini, Venturini and Vivaldi. Nowhere does Bach's name appear: the presentation score of the Brandenburg Concertos must have been included among either the '100 Concerte von diversen Meistern vor verschiedene Instrumente' or the '77 Concerte von diversen Meistern und für verschiedene Instrumente', where they were valued at 4 groschen each.

The Brandenburg Concertos were not, however, 'carelessly sold off among a lot of other instrumental concertos at a ridiculously low price', as Spitta put it.[24] Valuations were placed on the contents of the margrave's library not with a view to selling it but in order to ensure an equal distribution among the five beneficiaries of his estate, all of them members of the Prussian royal family. Which of the five came into possession of the Brandenburgs is not known, but the next owner of whom we have certain knowledge was the composer and theorist Johann Philipp Kirnberger (1721–83), who signed his name in the lower left-hand corner of the title-page (see Fig. 1). Kirnberger had been a pupil of Bach in Leipzig in 1739–40, and he remained an avid admirer and collector of his music. From 1752 he was active in Berlin, first in the royal *Kapelle* at Potsdam, then (from 1754) in the *Kapelle* of Prince Heinrich, and finally (from 1758) in the service of Princess Anna Amalia of Prussia (1739–1807), to whom he bequeathed the greater part of his important library. On Amalia's death it went with the rest of her rich collection to the Joachimsthalschen Gymnasium in Berlin (whose acquisition stamp can be seen in Fig. 1), and then in 1914 to the Royal Library, which was divided after World War II between East and West Berlin. The precious auto-graph of the Brandenburg Concertos is housed at present in the Deutsche Staatsbibliothek in Unter den Linden.

The available manuscript sources suggest that of the six Brandenburg Concertos only the fifth circulated at all widely during the period immediately following Bach's death. No doubt its solo harpsichord part

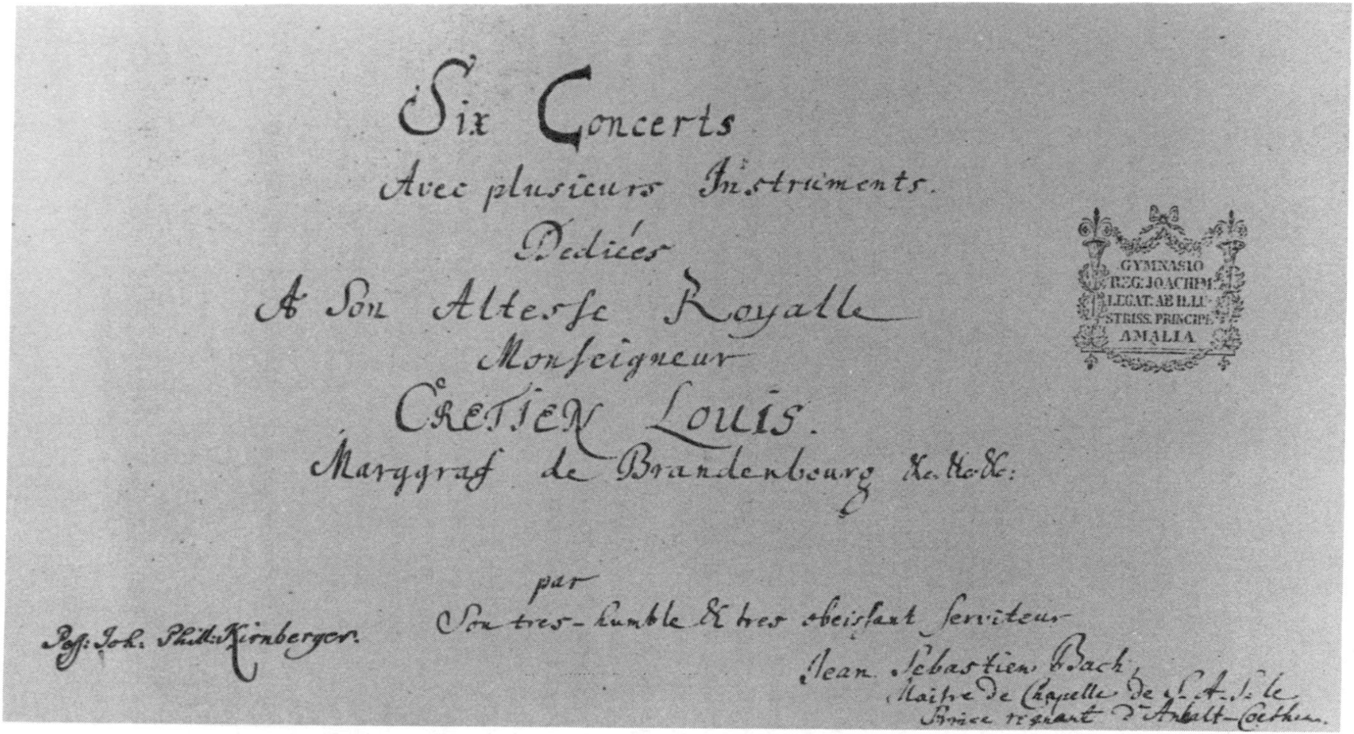

Fig. 1 Title–page of the Six Brandenburg Concertos (autograph); Deutsche Staatsbibliothek, Berlin, Amalien–Bibliothek n. 78

attracted attention at a time when the keyboard concerto was in the ascendancy; the instrumentation of most of the other concertos, by contrast, must have looked increasingly archaic as the standard Classical orchestra became firmly established in the major musical centres during the second half of the eighteenth century. The third concerto, however, could at least be played by the regularly constituted string section of the modern orchestra, even if the reinforcement of each line resulted in a less than ideal balance. One of the earliest public performances of a Brandenburg concerto during the first half of the nineteenth century (indeed, perhaps the first anywhere of which we have definite knowledge) took place at Frankfurt am Main on 19 May 1835, when Johann Nepomuk Schelble, a major figure in the nineteenth-century Bach revival, directed his Cäcilienverein in at least one movement of the third concerto. Before this, on 19 February 1808, Mendelssohn's teacher, Carl Friedrich Zelter, had included the fifth in one of the semi-private rehearsals he conducted for students and amateurs each Friday afternoon in Berlin. In 1813 the fourth and sixth were added to the repertory (the former becoming a firm favourite) and the second concerto was also played, at least until 1815.[25]

Mendelssohn himself apparently included none of the Bach concertos in his own concerts, and on the whole the Brandenburgs remained neglected and largely unknown. They had not been mentioned in the obituary that Bach's son Carl Philipp Emanuel and pupil Johann Friedrich Agricola wrote for Lorenz Mizler's *Musikalische Bibliothek* in 1754, nor in Forkel's biography of 1802, and it is not surprising to find that they had to wait until the centenary of Bach's death, in 1850, for publication. They were issued in that year by Peters of Leipzig in an edition by the German scholar Siegfried Wilhelm Dehn, who was responsible also for first editions of several other instrumental works by Bach.

Dehn was understandably excited by his rediscovery in 1849 of the autograph score in Princess Amalia's library, and he communicated this in letters to Ferdinand Roitzsch:

In the course of completing my catalogue of all J. S. Bach's works existing in Berlin, I have come across several compositions of the greatest importance which until now have remained entirely unknown (even to his sons C. P. E. and Wilh. Friedemann and to the scrupulous Forkel), including VI Concerti grossi, one of which is for p[iano]forte. [20 April 1849] and to the Austrian musicologist Aloys Fuchs:

At present I am concerned only with the J. S. Bach concertos; I have discovered several of them which – mirabile dictu! – are entirely unknown; among others are 6 (I repeat, six) Concerti grossi, and the rarities include the autographs of, for example, a concerto for piano with 2 oblig. flutes a bec!, a concerto for 2 violas and 2 viole da gamba with violone and cembalo, a concerto for violino piccolo (I have the proofs in front of me now), a concerto for 3 violins, 3 violas and 3 violoncelli etc., etc. [10 January 1850][26]

Dehn's preface to the first concerto is of particular interest as the earliest general description of these works to appear in print. He writes:

These six concertos, the first of which is now published with the others to follow shortly, have never before been made available in print.

The name of Johann Sebastian Bach is a guarantee of their high artistic merit and renders unnecessary any further recommendation. A comparison with the best examples of the genre by Bach's contemporaries – for example, with the concertos of Torelli, Corelli, Tartini, Vivaldi, Locatelli, Leclair and others – leads to the conviction that Johann Sebastian Bach has far surpassed them in these compositions, as he did also in others.

From a historical viewpoint, it is perhaps interesting to remark that some of these concertos are among the first, if not the very first, in which wind instruments are used, in addition to the strings, to accompany the soloists.

The information contained in the title which follows, and in the individual titles to each of the six concertos, all of which stem from Bach's own hand, will suffice for the present to draw the attention of the composer's many admirers to this notable undertaking on the part of a tireless publishing firm associated with many such offerings; it will also lead them to expect from the edition of these concertos the highest artistic enjoyment of a rare treasure.

Dehn based his edition on the autograph score, as also did Wilhelm Rust, whose edition for the *BG* served in its turn as the basis for several later editions of the whole set, including that of Arnold Schering (1927–9). Neither the editions of Dehn and Rust, however, nor the formation in 1850 of the Bach-Gesellschaft seem to have stimulated more frequent performances of the Brandenburg Concertos. Even the completion of the collected edition of Bach's works in 1900, and the founding that year of the Neue Bach-Gesellschaft, dedicated to promoting and performing the music, did little to alter the situation as far as the Brandenburgs were concerned. Max Reger's piano duet transcriptions, published by Peters in 1905–6, brought the concertos into the domain of domestic music-making, but the unusual, and by now exotic, instrumentation of the originals continued at first to inhibit conductors and impresarios from including them in public concerts. Performances which did take place were almost invariably in versions that adapted the instrumentation to the orchestras of the day and reinforced the string parts with as many players as the orchestra employed. The third and fifth concertos, which were the least problematical as far as their instrumentation was concerned, remained the most frequently performed.

It was largely with the gramophone record that the Brandenburg Concertos first became widely known, and this in turn stimulated more frequent concert performances. Recordings have in more recent times served to familiarize listeners with Bach's original instrumentation, but the very first recording of the complete set, made by the Busch Chamber Players directed by Adolf Busch in 1936, reflected what was normal practice in the concert hall at the time: the recorder parts in Nos. 2 and 4 were taken by flutes, the harpsichord solo in No. 5 (as well as the keyboard continuo in all the other concertos) was played on a piano, and cellos replaced the bass viols in No. 6.

The revival of interest in old instruments was already under way when Busch made these recordings: Arnold Dolmetsch had been making harpsichords, clavichords, lutes and viols for more than thirty years, and Wanda Landowska had been playing Bach on her huge Pleyel harpsichord for almost as long. But it was not until the early 1950s that the first recording on period instruments was made, by members of the Schola Cantorum Basiliensis directed by the Swiss conductor and viol player, August Wenzinger. (Wenzinger also published a performing edition of the concertos in 1959.) The next major landmark was the issue in 1959 of Thurston Dart's idiosyncratic recordings with the Philomusica of London (L'Oiseau-Lyre, SOL 60005–6). Dart argued for a reappraisal of Bach's instrumentarium in some of these works: he wanted *Jagdhörner*, sounding an octave higher than *Waldhörner*, for the first concerto (he actually used small trumpets in F in the recording) and flageolets for the wind parts in the fourth (though he settled for treble recorders in 1959). Dart's ideas, in fact, were only partly realized in the 1959 recording, but they surfaced again, more completely, in the recording he made with the Academy of St Martin in the Fields, conducted by Sir Neville Marriner, in 1971.[27] In this set horns are reinstated as the brass instruments in No. 1, and a horn, instead of a trumpet, is also used as a soloist in No. 2; sopranino recorders, sounding an octave higher than the written notes, replace Dart's first choice (flageolets) in No. 4.

Dart's theories caused something of a stir in musicological circles when his recordings were issued; they did at least concentrate attention on how best to meet Bach's requirements in these works, and the notes that Dart wrote to accompany the recordings were frequently discussed in the Bach literature (even if this was mainly to discredit them). Most of the more recent recordings that have aimed for an 'authentic' reading have adopted a more orthodox approach, taking advantage of the growing confidence that musicians have shown since 1959 in the playing of old instruments. With matters of text and instrumentation largely settled, it has been possible to concentrate again on personal interpretation – on the merits of, say, Leonhardt as compared with Koopman, of Harnoncourt compared with Pinnock. The recording that Christopher Hogwood made with the Academy of Ancient Music in 1985 (L'Oiseau-Lyre, 414 187), however, invites us to consider again the merits of the earlier versions of the first and fifth concertos compared with those of the margrave's score, which Hogwood feels 'carries a specious authority stemming more from its Dedication and calligraphy than from its value as source material'.

In the present writer's opinion, the historical value of Hogwood's recording of the Brandenburg Concertos lies mainly in his adoption of Laurence Dreyfus's views on what instruments Bach had in mind for his violone parts,[28] but perhaps the most important general lesson to be learnt from it is that there is seemingly no end to the theories and speculations that these fascinating works can engender.

3

Instrumentation

Bach probably intended the phrase 'avec plusieurs instruments' ('for several instruments'), in his title for the Brandenburg Concertos, as a French equivalent of the Italian 'a più stromenti' and similar designations found in such titles as Giovanni Lorenzo Gregori's *Concerti grossi a più stromenti* op. 2 (1698), Evaristo Felice Dall'Abaco's two sets of *Concerti a più istrumenti* opp. 5 (*c*.1719) and 6 (1735) and Carlo Tessarini's *Concerti a piu istrumenti* (*c*.1732, of doubtful authenticity). On the face of it the description 'a più stromenti' would seem superfluous: most concertos are for several instruments. What these collections have in common is that the instrumentation of the concertos they contain varies from work to work. (Dall'Abaco's first set has something else in common with Bach's in that it includes wind as well as string instruments.) The combination of 'grossi' and 'a più stromenti' in Gregori's title is unusual, perhaps unique; after 1700 the term 'concerto grosso' in published sets was increasingly reserved for works in the older Corellian tradition, in which the solo material was hardly differentiated from the tutti, while the more progressive Venetian type, with its greater opportunities for soloistic display, usually went under titles that specified the number of instrumental parts (though not necessarily the number of instruments) required: 'Concerti a quattro', 'Concerti a cinque' etc.[1]

The schoolroom definition of 'concerto grosso' as a concerto in which the solo group, or *concertino*, consists of more than one player simply will not do for the type (or types) of concerto that the Brandenburgs exemplify. Arthur Hutchings, whose pioneering study of the Baroque concerto has left all later students of the genre in his debt, has categorized the first, third and sixth Brandenburgs as 'ripieno concertos' and the others as 'concerti grossi'.[2] These are not definitions likely to find universal acceptance. The term 'ripieno concerto' may with some justification be used for the Third Brandenburg Concerto, since each member of the ensemble (except for the continuo players) is both soloist and a member of the tutti (or *ripieno*); but the sixth concerto is a kind of hybrid, with clearly identified solo and tutti components (but with the solo instruments fulfilling also a tutti role), while the first concerto, deriving from heterogeneous origins, is entirely *sui generis*. And to describe Nos. 2, 4 and 5 as 'concerti grossi' is to misapply a designation which Hutchings would surely not have used for, say, the concerto for two violins, BWV 1043, in which the solo–tutti disposition is fundamentally the same (and the same as that of the solo concertos as well). Bach's phrase 'avec plusieurs instruments' may seem vague, but it allies the Brandenburgs to the Venetian tradition stemming from Vivaldi and Albinoni just as firmly as Handel's 'Grand Concertos' places his op. 6 in the Corelli line, even if the concerto structures in both sets differ in many respects from those of their models.

There is, though, another sense in which Bach may be using the term 'plusieurs' here. In the *New Grove* article already referred to, Hutchings observed that '17th- [and 18th-]century publications advertised as "a più stromenti", including works by Giulio Taglietti, Dall'Abaco, Vitali and Henricus Albicastro, indicated their composers' wish for the sound of an orchestra, although they were prudently published as needing no more than one player to a part'.[3] Perhaps, then, Bach's intention was to indicate that his concertos require several, as distinct from many, players – in other words, one player to a part. Yet again, the term 'plusieurs instruments' might be interpreted as meaning 'several *different* instruments', since one of Bach's intentions in composing the Brandenburgs (or at least in putting them together as a set) seems to have been to embrace as wide a variety of instrumentation as possible.[4] All the instruments he writes for as soloists, with the exception of the harpsichord and perhaps the violino piccolo,[5] were also used as solo instruments in concertos by his contemporaries, but rarely, if ever, had so many different instruments been called for in a single set of concertos. The list is impressive (see Table 1).

The combination of wind and string instruments in a concerto is frequently referred to as a specifically German characteristic, but in fact Vivaldi also used various similar combinations, and four of his concertos (RV 568, 569, 571 and 574) have a rich assortment of instruments almost identical with those of the First Brandenburg Concerto. It is interesting, in view of this concerto's possible associations with the Saxon capital (see below, p. 73), that the instrumental parts of the four Vivaldi concertos have come down to us in manuscripts now in the Sächsische

Landesbibliothek, Dresden, with annotations in the hand of J. G. Pisendel, who was a violinist and later *Konzertmeister* there.

Table 1 *Instruments used in the Brandenburg Concertos*

Instrument as designated by Bach:	used (* as soloist) in concerto no.:
fiauto; fiauto d'echo [recorder]	2*, 4*
traversiere [flute]	5*
hautbois [oboe]	1*, 2*
bassono [bassoon]	1*
corno di caccia [horn]	1*
tromba [trumpet]	2*
violino [violin]	1, 2, 2*, 3*, 4, 4*, 5, 5*
violino piccolo	1*
viola	1, 2, 3*, 4, 5, 6*
viola da gamba [bass viol]	6
violoncello	1, 2, 3*, 4, 5, 6*
violone [double bass]	2, 3, 4, 5, 6
violono grosso [double bass]	1
cembalo [harpsichord][a]	[1], 2, 3, [4], 5*, 6

a The first and fourth concertos do not specify a 'cembalo', but its inclusion may be presumed under the designation 'continuo'.

Despite the immense amount of research that has been done this century on the construction and playing technique of eighteenth-century instruments, many problems about the instrumentation of the Brandenburg Concertos remain to perplex both the scholar and the performer. To take the instruments in the order in which they appear in the above list, one is immediately presented with the much-discussed question of whether the *fiauto* required for the second concerto is the same instrument as the two *fiauti d'echo* that Bach asks for in the fourth. It is universally agreed that the former is the treble recorder in F, a popular instrument in Bach's day by no means superseded by the new transverse flute; its part in the second concerto covers a compass from f' to g''' and is notated in what is commonly referred to as 'French violin clef' (a treble clef on the bottom line of the staff) to reduce the need for leger lines. Thurston Dart argued that the *fiauti d'echo* of the fourth concerto were flageolets of the type often used in the eighteenth century to train caged birds to sing or to imitate wild birds in vocal music, pitched in G and sounding an octave higher than written.[6] However, the compass, notation and technical demands of the *fiauti d'echo* parts are identical with those of the *fiauto* in the second concerto,[7] and it is worth noting also that Bach's curious designation for these instruments appears only in the concerto's title; in the score itself they are shown simply as 'fiauto 1mo' and 'fiauto 2do'. While acknowledging that the *f'* in bar 183 of the second part exceeds the lowest range of the flageolet, Dart rather disingenuously claims this as an oversight which Bach corrected by upwards transposition when he came to arrange the work as a harpsichord concerto in the 1730s. He fails to mention that the harpsichord version (BWV 1057) is in F major and that the passage in question would in any case have had to be altered to avoid the low *e♭'* unobtainable on the recorder; nor does he mention another low *f'* in the second *fiauto* part at bar 227.

If it is allowed that the solo woodwind instruments of the Fourth Brandenburg Concerto are indeed treble recorders, Bach's use of the term *fiauti d'echo* remains to be explained. It has often been suggested that it may refer to their role in the second movement, where, accompanied by the solo violin, they echo with *piano* phrases the *forte* statements of the full ensemble. But if this kind of explanation is looked for, the term could equally well refer to the way one recorder frequently 'echoes' the other in the first movement, either at the same pitch or in sequence. As Norman Carrell points out,[8] there is one passage in this movement where an 'echo' sequence is broken, and this provides further evidence for identifying the *fiauti* as treble recorders (see Ex. 2). It occurs three times in all, at bars 47–53, 275–81 and 391–7 of the first movement, and each time the second instrument leaps downwards to avoid the prominent top *f♯'''* which on the recorder is difficult to produce at speed or in tune, and would result in a feeble effect.[9]

Ex. 2   Brandenburg Concerto No. 4, first movement

The various explanations of 'fiauto d'echo' so far put forward were re-examined in 1992 by David Lasocki, who wrote in support of a hypothesis first suggested by John Martin, according to which an echo flute might have been made by 'fastening together a loud and a soft recorder'.[10] Lasocki quotes a passage from John Hawkins's *A General History of the Science and Practice of Music* (1776) in which the historian states that the younger John Banister (1662–1736) 'was famous for playing on two flutes [recorders] at once'. Lasocki argues that perhaps Hawkins meant to refer to James Paisible, a colleague of Banister, whose performances on the 'echo flute' between 1715 and 1719 were advertised in a number of London newspapers. Dart had already mentioned some of these London concerts and drew attention also to an advertisement in the *Daily Courant* for a benefit concert at Hickford's Rooms on 21 May 1716 for 'Signior Giorgio Giacomo Besivillibald, Servant to His Serene Highness the Margrave of Brandenburgh Anspach, Brother to H. R. H. Princess of Wales'. Dart argued that the margrave's musician might well have returned to Berlin with a couple of echo flutes (in his view, bird-flageolets) and that Bach may have heard these when he visited Berlin in 1719. But quite apart from the fact that the 'echo flutes' were more likely to have been the recorders to which Hawkins referred, both Dart and Lasocki confused Margrave Christian Ludwig with the Margrave of Brandenburg-Ansbach, who in 1716 was Wilhelm Friedrich (1685–1723).[11] The London connexion does not help us much in our attempts to solve the problem.

For the Fifth Brandenburg Concerto Bach turned to the single-key flute as it was developed by the Hotteterre family and other French makers in the seventeenth century. This was the instrument that was beginning to replace the recorder in popularity in Germany, as in other countries, and Bach writes for it over its fully chromatic two-octave compass, d' to d'''', and in its most effective and well-tuned key, D major. Unless the birthday cantata *Durchlauchtster Leopold* (BWV 173a) predates it, this concerto is Bach's earliest known composition for the instrument. Prince Leopold's collegium musicum included at least two musicians who played the 'flute' – Johann Gottlieb Würdig, a member of the *Kapelle* from 1714, and Johann Heinrich Freytag, who joined it in 1716 – but it is not known which of these (if either) played the transverse flute.

As recorder players, Würdig and Freytag are more likely, in fact, to have doubled on oboe than on the flute. Possibly they joined the oboist Johann Ludwig Rose on those occasions when the First Brandenburg Concerto was performed, in one version or another. The three oboes required in the definitive version of this work, as well as the single oboe that takes a solo part in the second concerto, are the standard instruments of the day, fitted with two keys to cover a fully chromatic range from c' to d''' which Bach again exploits to the full, carefully avoiding the low $c\sharp'$, which was difficult to obtain and of uncertain quality. As will be shown later (page 74), the earlier version of this work called for two oboes and a *taille*, or tenor oboe in F.

Only one of the Brandenburg Concertos – the first – calls for the bassoon. The 'Bassono' that Bach writes for is presumably the four-key instrument, capable of producing a low $G\sharp$, that was only just being developed in the early part of the century, rather than the older 'Fagotto' specified in several of the Weimar cantatas;[12] its compass here extends from C to $e\flat'$. Except for three half-bars in the first movement, the bassoon part doubles the continuo bass at the same pitch or (less often) at the octave in the first two movements; in the third movement, and again in the first trio of the minuet, it is clearly identified, following a French tradition stemming from Lully, as a bass for the oboes, but it never achieves the degree of independence it is given in, for example, the Sinfonia that introduces Cantata No. 42 (1725).

It is again only the First Brandenburg Concerto that includes horns (there are, as usual, two of them). These are the normal non-valved *corni di caccia* (specified thus in Bach's autograph) in F, capable of producing a diatonic, and partly chromatic, scale in the upper register, but only notes of the tonic triad and a flattened seventh in the lower range; the pitches (sounding a fifth lower) that Bach employs are shown in Ex. 3; those notated in black might have required some alteration in lip pressure to make them sound in tune.[13]

Ex. 3

The 'tromba' of Brandenburg Concerto No. 2 is more problematical. This is usually taken to be a trumpet in F sounding a perfect fourth above the notated pitch, and 'tromba' is indeed the word (along with 'clarino') normally used by Bach for the valveless trumpet of his day. Bach's other trumpet parts, however, are for instruments in C or D (a single exception being the E♭ trumpets required for the first version of the

Magnificat, BWV 243*a*); the questions raised by the trumpet part of the Second Brandenburg Concerto – which particular instrument Bach wrote for, who played it and which way it transposed (a fourth up or a fifth down) – still await convincing answers. The pitches Bach writes (in C) are shown in Ex. 4; in this case, too, the black notes would have challenged the player's technique to make them sound in tune. The balance of the evidence indicates that the part was indeed written for a trumpet in F sounding a fourth above the written notes; however, the designation 'Tromba ô vero Corno da Caccia' in the part copied by C. F. Penzel suggests that, after 1750 at least, performances may have been given on instruments sounding an octave lower than this. By the time the Brandenburg Concertos were revived and published in the nineteenth century the technique of virtuoso clarino playing had been lost. Siegfried Dehn, who was responsible for the first publication of the concertos in 1850, suggested that the trumpet part of No. 2 might be performed on a 'cornetto piccolo' in E♭; his alternative suggestion was even more radical: that the whole work should be transposed to D major and a high A trumpet used. It soon became commonplace to transfer some passages to a lower octave (as in Leopold Stokowski's recording with the Philadelphia Orchestra) or even to substitute entirely different instruments, such as a clarinet in C or E♭ and, later, a piccolo–heckelphone. According to Norman Carrell, Toscanini used a sopranino saxophone as late as 1950,[14] and Klemperer, in his recording with the Pro Musica of New York, divided the part between saxophone and clarinet. The first player to restore the high F trumpet for the part was evidently A. Goeyens in 1902; he also performed it on a piccolo trumpet in B♭.[15]

Ex. 4

Little need be said about the main members of the violin family: the violin itself, the viola and the cello. These are all familiar enough to modern audiences, and in outward appearance their Baroque forms differed only in such details as the length of the neck and fingerboard, the height of the bridge, the shape of the bow, and the absence of chin rests from violins and violas, and of spikes from cellos. (The effect of all these and other details of construction – the use of gut strings and a lighter bass-bar, for example – on the tone and playing technique of Baroque string instruments is, of course, a different matter, and one that twentieth-century interest in 'authentic' performance has taught us to appreciate.) The primacy of the violin as a concerto instrument during the late Baroque period is reflected in the fact that it appears as soloist in all the Brandenburg Concertos except the last, in which there are no violins at all. For the final version of the first concerto, however, Bach preferred a smaller type of violin, the violino piccolo, for reasons that will be suggested later. Surprisingly little is known about this instrument, and it is doubtful whether one can really speak about *the* violino piccolo as one might about *the* violin or *the* viola. All that can be said for certain about a violino piccolo is what the Italian term tells us: it was a small violin. Leopold Mozart referred to it as a concerto instrument:

Some years ago one even played concertos on the little violin (called by the Italians *Violino Piccolo*) and, as it was capable of being tuned to a much higher pitch than other violins it was often to be heard in company with a transverse flute, or harp, or other similar instruments. The little fiddle is no longer needed and everything is played on the ordinary violin in the upper registers.[16]

Since it is most unlikely that Leopold Mozart was acquainted with the First Brandenburg Concerto in 1756, one wonders which concertos with violino piccolo he is referring to here.

Most reference books give the instrument's tuning as a fourth higher than the normal violin, but the only accredited source of this information seems to be Michael Praetorius's tuning for the 'klein diskant Geig' in the second volume of his *Syntagma musicum* (Wolfenbüttel, 1619). Praetorius might well have been describing a tuning commonly found in a particular locality during a particular period; in all three works in which Bach uses the violino piccolo (Cantatas Nos. 96 and 140, in addition to the First Brandenburg Concerto) the instrument is tuned a minor third higher than the normal violin. It therefore functions as a transposing instrument, its part being notated a minor third lower than the pitch at which it is intended to sound.

The viol family that the violins had largely replaced by 1721 is represented in the sixth concerto by the inclusion of two bass viols. Bach uses the term 'viola da gamba', which strictly speaking could denote a viol of any size but must here refer to the six-string bass instrument, the only one of the family except for the violone in use in Germany during the eighteenth century. Bach uses the viols in this work mainly as accompanying instruments in the middle of the texture. The range of the second part extends over two octaves from Bb to bb'; that of the first exceeds this by one step in each direction. Bach makes no use of the instruments' low D string,[17] but on the other hand he asks the players to use a higher position on the top D string than he would normally expect from other accompanying string instruments (the viol's frets, of course, make the higher notes easier to negotiate than they are on the cello, for instance).

The question of which instrument Bach had in mind when he wrote a 'violone' part in the Brandenburg Concertos has been thoroughly examined by Laurence Dreyfus.[18] A violone is required in each of the six concertos (the first specifies a 'violono grosso'), but, despite attempts to identify an instrument which would serve for all six concertos,[19] it has long been apparent that more than one type of instrument is involved, since there are passages in the fourth and fifth concertos that indicate without any doubt that the violoni in those works could not reach the lowest notes that appear in the bass parts of some of the other concertos.[20] In fact, Dreyfus shows that the term 'violone' in the Brandenburg Concertos stands for three quite distinct instruments. For the first and third concertos the four-string *violone grosso* is needed, tuned in fourths (or sometimes in fifths) from its lowest string (C') and sounding an octave below the written pitch; the fourth and fifth concertos call for the six-string violone, tuned in fourths enclosing a major third one octave lower than the bass viol (thus not quite reaching down to the low C of the *violone grosso*) and again sounding an octave below the written notes; finally, the second and sixth concertos require what Daniel Speer[21] and other German writers of the period called the 'Bass-Violon' – a six-string violone tuned a fifth below the bass viol, with G' as its lowest note and sounding at the written pitch. Whether these observations can be used to bolster a particular chronology for the Brandenburg Concertos seems doubtful.

Finally there is the harpsichord, the instrument to which the Brandenburg Concertos in a sense owe their existence and which they, for the first time in the history of the concerto, elevated from the role of continuo instrument to that of soloist. We know little, if anything, about the harpsichords that Bach had at his disposal in Weimar and Cöthen before 1719, but we can be fairly certain about the type of instrument he went to collect from Berlin in that year, and for which he presumably wrote the solo part of the Fifth Brandenburg Concerto, at least in its final form. This was a two-manual instrument by Michael Mietke, perhaps the last one he made (he died in 1719); it remained in the princely *Kapelle* at

Cöthen until at least 1784, by which time it was apparently in need of repair.[22] As was mentioned in the previous chapter, two harpsichords almost certainly attributable to Mietke survive at the Schloss Charlottenburg in Berlin,[23] one of them a white, single-manual instrument decorated by the Flemish japanner Gerard Dagly, the other a two-manual instrument also decorated by Dagly (or by members of his workshop) on a black ground. Both harpsichords have been altered and their compass enlarged, but the two-manual instrument originally had one 4' and two 8' stops and a compass of F' to c''', without $F\sharp'$ and $G\sharp'$. To judge from the Fifth Brandenburg Concerto, the harpsichord that Mietke built for Cöthen had an identical upper limit to its compass but did not extend as far in the bass: only once, and only by a semitone, does the music descend below C. If Bach really did intend the final version of the concerto to show off the new instrument's capabilities he would surely have demonstrated a compass which exceeded the norm in Cöthen.

The harpsichord in the Fifth Brandenburg Concerto fulfils a dual role: when the right hand is silent it operates in the normal way as a continuo instrument, filling in the harmony from the figured bass. There is a touch of irony in the fact that it is only in this concerto, which promotes the harpsichord to the rank of soloist, that the bass is liberally and carefully figured in the autograph score. The reason for this is almost certainly that Bach intended the soloist to read from this score as he directed the ensemble, and to this end he made the solo part easily legible by writing it on staves which were more widely spaced than those for the other instruments (see Fig. 2).[24] In the other five concertos, where the keyboard instrument plays only an accompanying role, there are only seven notes in all that are figured. The figure 6 at bar 104 in the first movement of the second concerto serves to indicate the end of the *tasto solo* unison passage that marks the return of the main ritornello theme in the tonic; the figures at bars 107–11 in the same movement were perhaps called for to clarify the chromatic 'dominant' seventh and diminished seventh chords in that passage. A single example of figuring in the third movement of the first concerto (bar 18) is not so easy to account for.

One can hardly discuss the different instruments that Bach employs in the Brandenburg Concertos without also saying a word or two about the way he uses them in combination. To speak of 'orchestration', or even of 'instrumentation', in this connexion would be out of place, since the concept of 'scoring' as a process distinct from (though allied to)

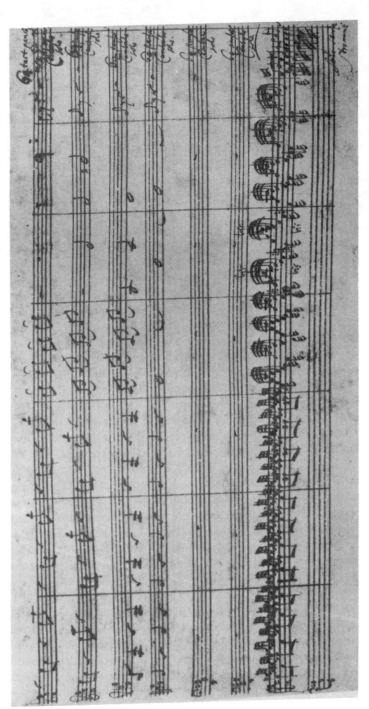

Fig. 2 Brandenburg Concerto No. 5, first movement, bars 148–54 (autograph); Deutsche Staatsbibliothek, Berlin, Amalien-Bibliothek n. 78

composition is one that belongs to a later age. (The earliest manual devoted entirely to orchestration, Jean-Georges Kastner's *Traité général d'instrumentation*, did not appear until 1837; Berlioz's famous *Grand traité d'instrumentation et d'orchestration modernes* was published six years later.) The instrumentarium of the Brandenburg Concertos is not as large or as varied as that of the church cantatas taken as a whole, but in bringing together 'plusieurs instruments' in these six works Bach does seem to have been intent on showing the paces of as wide a variety as possible of instruments, both current and obsolescent, in the concerto genre. Despite this, two norms of late Baroque concerto scoring may be observed. One of these is the employment of the standard four-part string group of first and second violins, viola, bass (cello and violone) and continuo for the *ripieno* component in three out of the six works. The third and sixth concertos are, of course, special cases in this respect; whether the unusual omission of a second violin from the *ripieno* of the fifth concerto can be accounted for by Bach's relinquishing his customary desk among the strings in order to play the demanding solo part is something that has frequently been discussed, but never resolved. The other norm is the polarization of soloist(s) and bass in the episodes of ritornello movements – though this is not nearly as prominent as it is in the concertos of Vivaldi, or for that matter in those of Bach's German contemporaries.

What is much more difficult to talk about is the relationship between the scoring of the Brandenburg Concertos and the expression, or more simply the fabric, of the music. Bach was as sensitive as any of his contemporaries to the expressive connotations of particular instruments. He was well aware of the effectiveness of trumpets for imposing ceremonial music, of horns for hunting scenes, flutes and recorders for pastoral contexts, and viols for sentiments associated with death and mourning. But how far the choice of instruments in non-vocal pieces was influenced by considerations of 'colour' or 'expression' in the music is by no means clear. It is often pointed out, for example, that the absence of violins and other high-pitched instruments from Brandenburg Concerto No. 6 results in a distinctively 'dark' or 'veiled' tonal hue, which is emphasized by the inclusion of bass viols. But there is no need to suppose that this particular instrumental colouring was an essential part of Bach's conception of the work; one could argue that the music would be just as well served by an ensemble which included violins, flutes and oboes (in a key which suited the instrumentation, of course). It seems quite likely that the availability of players was more decisive in the choice of instruments than any desire to colour the music in a particular and unusual way.

Apart from this concerto and also the fifth of the set, with its innovative inclusion of the harpsichord as a solo instrument, it is the Second Brandenburg Concerto that has elicited most comment for its instrumentation. Here Bach projects a seemingly ill-matched combination of trumpet, recorder, oboe and violin against the standard *ripieno* complement of four-part strings and continuo. Leaving aside for the moment the question of which particular instrument Bach had in mind for the 'tromba' part, the instrumentation here speaks volumes, not only about the composer's approach to this aspect of his craft but also about the purpose served by a piece of late Baroque music. The scoring excites comment both for the unusual combination of solo instruments and for the way that Bach writes for them. Even after allowing for the differences in dynamic range and tone quality between the instruments of Bach's time and those of a modern orchestra, and after taking into consideration the difference between a princely salon and a modern concert hall, it must be acknowledged that the solo instruments brought together in the Second Brandenburg Concerto are not calculated to produce the kind of blend and balance that a nineteenth- or early twentieth-century composer would have thought of as a hallmark of good instrumentation. A quite different aesthetic is conveyed in the scoring of the first solo episode of the opening movement, in which the violin's *bariolage* accompaniment to the oboe's version of the theme is taken up first by the oboe itself and then by the recorder as the theme passes to the other instruments in turn (see Ex. 5; see also Ex. 16, p. 76). It is obvious from this passage, and others

Ex. 5   Brandenburg Concerto No. 2, first movement

like it, that idiomatic instrumental writing (a *sine qua non* of any competent orchestrator in a later age) has no high priority in Bach's thinking as a composer. This is not to say, of course, that he writes for the trumpet exactly as he writes for the recorder, or for the oboe as he writes for the violin. But on the whole it seems to be an instrument's limitations (the trumpet's inability to play notes outside the harmonic series; the impossibility of playing chords on wind instruments) rather than its inherent qualities that determine the demands that Bach makes on it. When composing a piece like the Second Brandenburg Concerto, Bach's first thoughts would have been for those who were to play it rather than for those who were to listen. Quite probably they were the same people anyway.

4

The dedication score and its design

The standard format for instrumental publications, including concertos, in the eighteenth century was a set of six or twelve pieces, usually under a single opus number. Vivaldi's published concertos were all issued in sets of either six or twelve (those with twelve being printed in two books of six concertos each), and Bach followed the same practice in his relatively few published works except for those, such as the *Art of Fugue* and the *Musical Offering*, in which some other ordering principle prevailed. Bach's keyboard partitas, although issued separately at first, were published as a set of six in 1731; there are also six organ chorales in the 'Schübler' collection of 1748/9. Even when there was no immediate prospect of publication, Bach followed the practice of bringing his instrumental works to a final form in groups of six. The English and French Suites for keyboard, the organ sonatas BWV 525–30, the sonatas for violin and harpsichord BWV 1014–19, the sonatas and partitas for solo violin and the suites for solo cello all exemplify this, as also do the six Brandenburg Concertos.

The dedication score of the Brandenburg Concertos, which is in Bach's own hand almost throughout,[1] has, then, the same validity and standing as a print, but allowances should be made for the fact that Bach could not, of course, make the kind of corrections he would undoubtedly have made on a printer's proof. He did, in fact, make numerous errors in preparing the dedication score, partly because in some instances he was not merely transcribing the music but at the same time revising it. Sometimes the error is still perceptible beneath a corrected note; in other cases the correct reading is conveyed by note names written above the staff.[2] Such errors have sometimes been cited as evidence for the view that the margrave did not have the musicians to perform these concertos; Bach, it is argued, was well aware of this and therefore took no great care in the accuracy of the dedication score. The state of the manuscript as a whole does not support this, however; only in a few cases has an error gone unnoticed and uncorrected.

In most respects the dedication copy betokens great care in its preparation. Bach, or his assistant, was assiduous in ruling just the right number of staves for the particular concerto or movement to be copied, even if the composer's second thoughts have resulted, in at least one instance, in a less than wholly satisfactory layout on the page.[3] Each staff has been ruled individually, and yet the ruled staves rarely depart much from the parallel. It is evident from the fact that the lowest space on each staff is almost consistently greater than the others, that a single rastrum has served to rule the staves for the first four concertos (see Fig. 3), for most of the fifth and perhaps for the sixth as well. For the harpsichord part of the fifth concerto, however, Bach went to the trouble of using a second, broader rastrum (see Fig. 2), but, for reasons which will be explained later, he found himself obliged to modify the layout of the manuscript for the cadenza and for the second movement. For the staves of the final movement only the main, narrower rastrum was used, which suggests, as Christoph Wolff pointed out, that Bach broke off the copying after the slow movement and then forgot to adopt again the unusual, but essentially practical, format of the first movement when he resumed work on the manuscript.[4] By the time he came to copy the sixth concerto he had evidently either had some repairs made to the main rastrum or discarded it for another. The staff lines for this concerto are much more evenly spaced, though not consistently so.

The bar-lines were no less carefully drawn than the staves, always (except in the cadenza of the fifth concerto) with a ruler and mostly a page or two in advance. Occasionally Bach misjudged the space he would need for a particular passage and had to squeeze the notes in or allow them to spill over into another bar (see Fig. 2); in more extreme cases, or when a folio had to be discarded for some reason, he might be forced to erase some of the prepared bar-lines.

Prior to the ruling of staves and bar-lines, of course, must have come the decision about which works to include and in what order. An unusual feature of the Brandenburg Concertos as a set (indeed a unique one as far as Bach is concerned) is that they are all in major keys; in each of the other half-dozen sets the composer mixes major and minor in the proportion 4:2 (the cello suites), 2:4 (the English Suites) or 3:3 (the others). There can be no doubt that the prevailing major mode in the Brandenburg Concertos contributes to the joyous, outgoing quality that

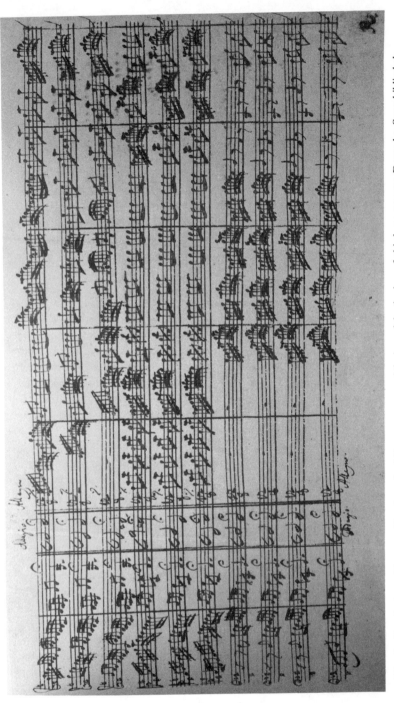

Fig. 3 Brandenburg Concerto No. 3: end of first movement, Adagio and beginning of third movement; Deutsche Staatsbibliothek, Berlin, Amalien-Bibliothek, n. 78

the modern listener finds in the music, though it would be a mistake to make simplistic equations between major/minor modality and a composer's expressive intentions in Baroque music. Another unique feature of the Brandenburgs is that it is Bach's only instrumental set in which any key appears more than once, both F major and G major being duplicated in the first four concertos.

One can only speculate on Bach's reasons for placing the concertos in the particular order in which they appear in the presentation copy (the only surviving source, incidentally, to include all six works). Possibly he put BWV 1046 first because he reckoned that its stylistic allegiance to the French orchestral suite might commend it to the frenchified taste of the Berlin court (the dedication, it will be remembered, was in courtly French). The coupling of concertos with key signatures of one flat and one sharp would then follow more or less as a matter of course, to be followed by those with two sharps and flats (the B♭ major concerto, rather than the D major one, placed last so that each half of the collection would end with a concerto for strings alone). It is probably not accidental, then, that the two string concertos (Nos. 3 and 6) divide the set into two halves, and it is worth observing that No. 3 is for three groups of three instruments (plus continuo), while No. 6 is for six instruments (counting violone and cembalo as a single continuo component; they share the sixth staff in the score).

While diversity seems to have been Bach's overriding concern in the instrumentation of these concertos, as we have seen, they do also exhibit a degree of uniformity in other respects, and this might encourage us to see them as a group rather than a miscellany. Except for the first concerto, which has every appearance of having been 'manufactured' from non-concerto material expressly for inclusion in the set, each work is in the standard Italianate three-movement form of two quick movements separated by a slow one (this applies even to the third concerto, with its 'missing' Adagio), and in each case the slow movement is in the relative minor key (that of the last concerto, however, begins in the subdominant major). Ritornello form is the norm for the fast movements – though, as might be expected, Bach approaches it in an adventurous and innovative way.

Thematic integration, whether between the movements of a concerto or between different concertos, almost certainly played no part in Bach's composition of these works or in his decision to bring them together under one cover. It is nevertheless striking to observe how many main themes, particularly opening themes, share a family resemblance either through the prominent use of an arpeggiated tonic chord (*x*) or through the inclusion of a three-note figure (*y*), usually on the pitches tonic–leading-note–tonic (or *doh'–te–doh'*); not infrequently both tonic chord and three-note figure are present simultaneously (see Ex. 6).

Ex. 6   (a) No. 1, first movement

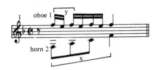

(b) No. 2, first movement

(c) No. 3, first movement

(d) No. 3, third movement

(e) No. 4, third movement

(f) No. 5, first movement

(g) No. 6, first movement

(h) No. 6, first movement

(i) No. 6, third movement

(j) No. 6, third movement

Needless to say, it can have been no part of Bach's design that the six concertos should be performed as a group. Their inclusion together in a modern recording is understandable enough, but to present them complete in a single evening in the concert hall, as is sometimes done nowadays, leaves many of the musicians underemployed and is perhaps not in the best interests of the audience either.

5

The ritornello structure

The term 'ritornello' (a diminutive of the Italian *ritorno*, meaning 'return') has a long history which can be traced back at least to fourteenth-century Italian verse forms. Its appearance in musical scores dates from the early seventeenth century, when composers began to use it for an instrumental section repeated at various points in the course of a vocal composition such as an opera. Monteverdi's *Orfeo* (1607) provides several examples. Towards the end of the century the term appeared frequently in the cantatas and operas of Alessandro Scarlatti and his contemporaries to denote an orchestral introduction or (more often) a coda to an aria in which the singer was accompanied only by the basso continuo, but it seems not to have been much used at this time with reference to concertos. The entry 'Ritornello' in J. G. Walther's *Musicalisches Lexicon* (1732), for instance, makes no mention of the genre, and neither do the corresponding entries in the musical dictionaries of Sébastien de Brossard (1703) and James Grassineau (1740). J. J. Quantz's consistent use of 'Ritornello' in the references he makes to the concerto in his *Versuch einer Anweisung die Flöte traversiere zu spielen* (1752) seems to be untypical.

In fact, it is only in comparatively recent times that the term 'ritornello' has come into general use to denote the opening tutti and its subsequent reappearances in a Baroque concerto. German scholars writing during the Bach revival in the second half of the nineteenth century preferred a terminology derived from Classical sonata form, with which they were more familiar. Spitta, for example, speaks of the 'Tutti-Thema' and the solo entry as corresponding to the first and second subjects in sonata form;[1] in his account of the Brandenburg Concertos he uses the terms 'Exposition' and 'Durchführung' ('working-out' or 'development'), but never 'ritornello'.[2] A similar approach can be observed until far into the twentieth century in analyses of Bach's concerto movements by such writers as August Halm (1919) and Walther Krüger (1932).[3] Krüger proposed the terms 'Thesis' and 'Antithesis' for the opening ritornello and first episode respectively; together they formed the 'Exposition', which was then subject to a series of different developments ('Durch-führungen'), the movement ending with a 'Reprise' of the Thesis. Rudolf Gerber (1951) does occasionally use 'Ritornell', but prefers '*Tutti*themen' or '*Tutti*abschnitte' and continues to employ the term 'Durchführungen' for reappearances of these and the 'Solothemen'.[4] As recently as 1981 the Soviet musicologist Vladimir Protopopov preferred 'Eingang"satz"'[3] to 'Ritornell' in the German version of his paper on the da capo principle in Bach's Concertos.[5]

German scholars have not been alone in their reluctance to adopt the term 'ritornello' in writings on the Baroque concerto. Among English writers in the first half of the twentieth century, Donald Tovey understood perfectly its relevance to Bach's concertos,[6] but while the article 'Ritornello' in the fifth edition of *Grove's Dictionary* (1954) included a definition of its function in the concerto, those in the fourth (1940) and earlier editions did not. Neither J. A. Fuller-Maitland (for whom the Bach concerto structure had 'a place of some importance in the development of that beautiful plan, known as the 'sonata form', which reigned supreme in classical music from Haydn to Brahms') nor Norman Carrell so much as mentions the term in the books they published on the Brandenburg Concertos in 1929 and 1963 respectively.[7] This is especially surprising in the case of Carrell's book, as the term 'ritornello' had by 1963 become widely used among English-speaking musicians, thanks largely to the writings of Manfred Bukofzer and Arthur Hutchings.[8]

As Michael Talbot has written, ritornello form was 'the quasi-automatic choice for the first movement in a Vivaldi concerto ... [and] the most common choice for finales'.[9] This applies equally well to the concertos of Bach, and more than half of the eighteen movements in the Brandenburg Concertos (including all six first movements) are in some kind of ritornello form. Indeed, the potential of the ritornello structure was perhaps the most important lesson that Bach learnt from his great Italian predecessor. As might be expected, Bach developed and elaborated the ritornello idea more than any other composer before Mozart, but his highly personal, original and far-reaching innovations are best understood if we approach them from the 'classical' structure as we find it in the mature works of Vivaldi and his Italian contemporaries.

Fundamental to ritornello structure is the alternation of a passage containing the basic thematic substance of the movement (ritornello) with others in which the music is largely or wholly new (episodes). In the 'classical' structure the ritornello, heard in full and in the tonic key at the beginning, returns in related keys and usually in truncated form at various points during the course of the movement, and again in the tonic, and usually complete, at the end. The episodes are more dynamically conceived, effecting a move from the key of one ritornello to that of the next. The structure may be thought of, and most probably originated as, an extension of the first section of the da capo aria and, as has already been mentioned, it is no coincidence that both Vivaldi and Albinoni were known in Venice principally as opera composers. In the da capo aria, which since the 1680s had prevailed in Venetian opera (as it had elsewhere) almost to the exclusion of any other type, the music and text of the first part were repeated after the second, in which the remainder of the text was usually set more briefly and without instrumental ritornellos. The result was a simple ternary form, ABA. Since the da capo structure as an entity is not without relevance to the concerto, as we shall see, it might conveniently be summarized here as follows:[10]

Section:	Rit	A	Rit	A'	Rit	B	(da capo)
Keys (major):	I......	I $\longrightarrow$	V......	V $\longrightarrow$	I......	vi $\longrightarrow$ iii	(da capo)
Keys (minor):	i......	i $\longrightarrow$	III.....	III $\longrightarrow$	i......	? $\longrightarrow$ v	(da capo)
				fine			

The most obvious distinction between this structure and the ritornello movement of a concerto is the aria's overall ternary design – although this is, in fact, found in some of Bach's concerto movements, as also, independently, is the typical iii–I or v–i tonal switch that marks the return of the ritornello theme after the B section. There is, however, another structural distinction to be drawn between the aria and the concerto movement, and this one is far less obvious, though it should always be borne in mind when making comparisons between vocal and instrumental movements of this kind. It may seem in an aria that the first vocal solo derives its thematic material from the opening ritornello, but of course it is the text that will have determined the tempo, metre, rhythm, accentuation, phrase-lengths and often the very pitches of that ritornello material. In other words, it is the soloist's entry that is conceived first, even though the ritornello theme is the first thing to be heard, and may even have been the first thing the composer actually wrote down.[11] In the concerto the reverse applies. Composition begins with the ritornello, and as a result the episode material is usually much more independent of it than is the case in an aria.

While on the subject of the da capo aria, Bach's highly individual use in cantatas and other vocal works of what has often been called the 'free da capo' structure must be mentioned, since this also impinges on the design of some of his concerto movements in one way or another. 'Free' is, in fact, an inaccurate and misleading term to describe the carefully calculated and forward-looking structure one encounters in most of these arias.[12] In them the first A section closes not in the tonic but in the dominant (or dominant minor); after the B section the text of A is repeated to basically the same music as before, beginning in the tonic but recomposed so as to close in the tonic as well. The A-major aria 'Wohl euch, ihr auserwählten Seelen' from Cantata No. 34, *O ewiges Feuer, o Ursprung der Liebe*, exemplifies the type very clearly.[13] It can be represented diagrammatically as follows:

	'exposition'							'recapitulation'		
Section:	Rit	A	Rit	B	Rit	B'		Rit	A'	Rit
Keys:	I......	I $\longrightarrow$	V......	V $\longrightarrow$	vi......	vi $\longrightarrow$ iii		I......	I......	I
Bar nos.:	1	9	23	30	34	40	44	45	48	66(–72)

As far as tonality is concerned, it will be seen that the first A section is related to its repeat (A') in much the same way as the exposition of a Classical sonata-form movement is related to the recapitulation. Except in its proportions and lack of thematic differentiation, the structure is in fact very close to that found in the first movements of some early concertos by Bach's son Carl Philipp Emanuel. A structure closer to the generality of ritornello movements in late Baroque concertos (including Bach's) is found in those arias that dispense with the textual da capo, and therefore with the incentive to reinstate the tonic key before the final ritornello.[14]

The 'classical' type of ritornello in the concertos of Vivaldi and Bach is one for which Wilhelm Fischer invented the term 'Fortspinnungstypus'.[15] The ritornello itself comprises a motivic *Vordersatz* which immediately establishes the key and character of the movement and is easily recognizable on its return; a *Fortspinnung*, or continuation, usually involving sequential repetition; and a cadential *Epilog*. The opening of the Third Brandenburg Concerto exemplifies the type quite well, although one might argue about where exactly the *Fortspinnung* ends and the *Epilog* begins (see Ex. 7).[16] As an analytical crutch the idea of the *Fortspinnungstypus* should not be relied upon in every situation, especially perhaps in

Ex. 7   Brandenburg Concerto No. 3, first movement

analysing Bach's concerto movements, but it does provide a convenient terminology in many cases. The ritornello of the first movement of the fifth concerto also shows the threefold division quite clearly, but others are altogether more complicated. Some embody fugal procedures (see below); in the first movement of the sixth concerto the *Vordersatz*, *Fortspinnung* and *Epilog* seem to be telescoped into a single unit defined by the rounded, slowly changing harmonic progression over which it unfolds; the opening ritornello of the fourth concerto, on the other hand, is extended to 83 bars by a threefold statement of the *Vordersatz* (in tonic, dominant and again tonic), each one succeeded by a different *Fortspinnung*, so that the whole section fulfils the ambiguous function of a ritornello on the one hand and the A section of a large-scale ternary (da capo) form on the other – an ambiguity reinforced by the independent activity of the soloists during the ritornello and by the mediant (B minor) cadence that precedes its exact repeat at the end of the movement.

This invasion by the soloists of what is traditionally the domain of the tutti (whether we think of this as an orchestra or as an ensemble) is worth commenting on, since it is by no means as common in Bach's concertos as is sometimes made out. A few instances of brief soloistic interventions in opening ritornellos can be found in other works, it is true (the E major Violin Concerto furnishes a well-known example, and the F minor Harpsichord Concerto another), but in the ritornello movements of the Brandenburg Concertos the integrity of the tutti is in nearly every other case preserved, either by the soloists' remaining silent or by their doubling the tutti lines. The exceedingly small ensemble of the sixth concerto rules out the possibility of any doubling between soloists and tutti in that work, but the ritornellos of the third movement are clearly defined by having the two solo violas double each other. The first movement of the second concerto is, of course, a special case, since the notes available to the solo trumpet make it impossible for it to double other instruments. The first movement of the first concerto might appear to constitute another exception, but this was almost certainly not conceived as a concerto movement and does not easily lend itself to analysis on concerto lines.

The most profound difference between the concerto allegros of Vivaldi and those of Bach lies in the relationship between ritornello and episode and between tutti and soloist(s) (the terms are not, strictly speaking, interchangeable). Whereas in Vivaldi's approach, at least as far as the violin concertos are concerned, it is usually contrast between the two elements that is the prime consideration, Bach's concern is more for integration. Thus in the typical Vivaldian episode the texture is reduced to one of soloist and continuo (or upper strings in unison), with perhaps brief interjections of ritornello material from the tutti. Although the musical material itself may sometimes be derived from some phrase in the ritornello, it is the novel and virtuoso figuration of the soloist that catches the ear. The outer movements of the Second and Fourth Brandenburg Concertos also provide several examples of passages in which the *ripieno* is reduced to continuo only (and some, indeed, where it is completely silent), but Bach's episodes are on the whole much more richly textured than Vivaldi's, with the string group largely taking over the continuo's accompanying role. In terms of thematic content, too, Bach's episodes are more eventful, with references to ritornello material becoming the norm rather than the exception.

Integration of ritornello and episode in the Bach concertos is achieved in other ways, too. In a Vivaldi concerto the return of the ritornello after an episode is usually quite obvious to the listener: the reintroduction of the full string band, playing, as a rule, the arresting opening gesture of the movement, makes it an event not to be missed. Similarly, the end of the ritornello will be strongly punctuated, if not by the original *Epilog*, at least by a well-defined cadence. In Bach's case the endings of ritornellos are in most cases similarly articulated, but often an episode will merge imperceptibly into a return of ritornello material in a way which takes the listener unawares. This is, of course, partly because of the relatively little textural differentiation between ritornellos and episodes, but it can result also from Bach's way of reintroducing the ritornello not with the *Vordersatz*, but with *Fortspinnung* material, and with dominant rather than tonic harmony. The result is an extremely fluent and unpredictable structure, in which the interests of continuity and of contrast are nicely balanced. It is seen at its subtlest, perhaps, in the opening movement of the Fourth Brandenburg Concerto.

Michael Talbot mentions the Concerto for Three Violins, RV 551, as an instance of Vivaldi's thematic linking of the first and last episodes in a ritornello movement.[17] Such restatements of episodic material, exceptional in the Vivaldi concertos, become the norm in Bach's ritornello schemes. Indeed, there is not a single instance of any Bach movement of this type in which every episode is thematically independent of the others (although the first movement of the F minor Harpsichord Concerto, BWV 1056 – probably among his earliest examples of the genre – comes close to providing an exception). Of the ritornello movements in the Brandenburgs, the one that shows the greatest variety in its episodes (and, incidentally, the one in which the episodes are thematically most independent from the ritornello) is probably the first movement of the fourth concerto, but even here the first part of the second episode (bars 165–85) is recalled later in the movement (bars 285–310). Of particular interest are those movements in which an episode modulates from tonic to dominant on its first appearance and later returns modified in such a way as to end in the tonic. A clear example is provided by the first movement of the Sixth Brandenburg Concerto, where the first episode (bars 17–25, modulating from B♭ to F) is exactly recalled at bars 103–10, except that the closing bars are now altered to reach a cadence in the tonic; the same relationship exists in the first movement of the fifth concerto, when the first episode at bars 9–19 is recalled at bars 110–21. Bach's practice in such instances almost certainly stems from the 'exposition–recapitulation' relationship found in many of his so-called free da capo arias (see p. 48, above).

It would be quite impossible to point to any movement, least of all in the Brandenburg Concertos, as being typical of Bach's handling of ritornello structure, but we may gain some idea of both the mastery and the diversity he brings to it by looking closely at one of the most straightforward and then at one of the most complex movements in this form. It is not surprising, perhaps, that for the former the choice should fall on a slow movement, where some relaxation in compositional activity is appropriate to the musical expression. Vivaldi's employment of the ritornello idea in a slow tempo is virtually confined to those movements in which an initial and concluding tutti passage (often in bare octaves) acts as a kind of frame for a through-composed movement for the soloist (or soloists) with light accompaniment; one familiar example among many is the middle movement of the Violin Concerto in D, RV 230, which is one of those that Bach arranged for solo harpsichord (as BWV 972).

The Adagio of Bach's D minor Harpsichord Concerto, BWV 1052, is also framed by a string 'ritornello' in octaves (which Bach typically makes use of in the bass throughout the movement), but 'ritornello form' is not really any more appropriate a designation for this than it is for Vivaldi's movements of this type. Of the five slow movements in the Brandenburg Concertos, only that of No. 5 can truly be said to be in ritornello form and, paradoxically, it is one of those in which the tutti ensemble is silent. Here the ritornellos are defined, firstly, by having the solo harpsichord perform a continuo role from a figured bass; secondly, by a change of dynamic in the flute and violin parts from *piano* for the episodes to *forte* for the ritornellos; and thirdly, by a return of the initial figure (Ex. 8a) in a new key. The episodes are characterized by the right hand of the harpsichord joining the flute and violin as soloist, and by a gently lulling figure whose paired semiquavers contrast with the bold dotted rhythms of the opening (Ex. 8b); both figures lend themselves to inversion. The only time when this sharp division of labour is eroded is in the fourth ritornello, where the return of the initial theme in G major is preceded by two bars, beginning in E minor, derived from the episode theme. The structure of the movement is summarized in Table 2. Within its relatively modest scope, this movement is impressive for its compositional resource and its satisfying proportions. Practically all the material is derived from the two short fragments quoted in Ex. 8, which find their fullest working-out in the last, and longest, of the four episodes. Despite the absence of the string ensemble, the ritornello structure is clearly articulated.

Ex. 8   Brandenburg Concerto No. 5, second movement

Altogether more complex and exploratory in its use of ritornello form (and, with 427 bars, one of the longest of all Bach's concerto movements) is the opening Allegro of Brandenburg Concerto No. 4. The exceptional length (eighty-three bars) of its initial ritornello and the participation in it of the solo instruments have already been mentioned. A threefold statement of the *Vordersatz* (in the tonic, dominant and again tonic), each time followed by a different *Fortspinnung*, results in an unusually eventful

Table 2 *Brandenburg Concerto No. 5: 2nd movement (Affettuoso)*

Bar nos.(total)	Ritornello/Episode	Tonality	Comments
1–5 (5)	Ritornello 1	B min	violin leads
5–10 (5)	Episode 1	B min–D maj	
10–14 (4)	Ritornello 2	D maj	flute leads
14–20 (6)	Episode 2	D maj–F♯ min	inversion of figures *x* and *y* (see Ex. 8)
20–24 (4)	Ritornello 3	F♯ min	transposition of Ritornello 1; flute leads
24–30 (6)	Episode 3	F♯ min–E min	extension of Episode 1; harpsichord leads
30–34 (4)	Ritornello 4	E min–G maj	uses figures *y* and *x*; flute leads
34–45 (11)	Episode 4	G maj–B min	recalls Episode 2 (with exchange between flute and violin); extended by *y* in *recto* (flute and violin) and inversion (harpsichord) accompanied by *x* (bass)
45–9 (4)	Ritornello 5	B min	exact repetition of Ritornello 1

ritornello from which at least five distinct motifs can be isolated (see Ex. 9). Cohesion results largely from a downward arpeggio figure (*x*) which occurs either as part of each motif (except the last) or as a counterpoint to it, and the ritornello is clinched with an *Epilog* of syncopated antiphony which serves to emphasize each structural modulation. Downward (and later upward) arpeggios characterize the first episode, too (Ex. 10a), but with the recorders' dialogue in the second episode (where, it will be noted, one instrument 'echoes' the other) stepwise movement begins to prevail (Ex. 10b), and this is maintained in the rushing scales with which the violin succeeds in masking some clever close canon between recorders and orchestral violins (bars 197–208). Close canon between solo and orchestral violins, sometimes *à*3, is continued in episode three (Ex. 10c), punctuated by reminiscences of the ritornello *Vordersatz* and passages of solo figuration from episode one. The final episode recalls the second, and the movement ends, after a cadence in the mediant minor, with a complete return of the opening ritornello. The movement's structure is summarized in Table 3.

Ex. 9 Brandenburg Concerto No. 4, first movement

Ex. 9 cont.

(e) [Epilog]

recorders

strings and continuo

Ex. 10   Brandenburg Concerto No. 4, first movement

(a) violin

(b) recorders

(c) solo violin

violin 1 *pp*

violin 2 *pp*

cello, violone and continuo

Bach's enrichment of the Vivaldian ritornello design can be observed also in movements that combine it with other structures and textures, particularly those of the da capo aria and the fugue. An archetypal example of da capo structure is provided by the last movement of Brandenburg Concerto No. 6, in which the entire first section (bars 1–45),

Table 3 *Brandenburg Concerto No. 4: 1st movement (Allegro)*

Bar nos. (total)	Ritornello/Episode	Motifs	Keys	Remarks
1–83 (83)	Ritornello 1	*a, b, c, d, e*	G maj	for motifs see Ex. 9
1–13 (13)	*Vordersatz*	*a*	[G maj]	
13–23 (10)	*Fortspinnung 1*	*b*	[G–D maj]	
23–35 (13)	*Vordersatz*	*a*	[D maj]	
35–57 (22)	*Fortspinnung 2*	*c, b*	[G maj]	
57–69 (13)	*Vordersatz*	*a*	[G maj]	
69–79 (10)	*Fortspinnung 3*	*d*	[G maj]	
79–83 (4)	*Epilog*	*e*	[G maj]	
83–137 (54)	Episode 1		G maj–E min	
83–125 (42)	new material		[G–D maj]	solo violin; see Ex. 10a
125–37 (12)	*Fortspinnung*	*c*	[D maj–E min]	ritornello motif (tutti)
137–57 (21)	Ritornello 2	*a, d, e*	E min	
157–209 (52)	Episode 2		E min–C maj	
157–85 (28)	new material		[E min–A min]	recorders; see Ex. 10b; includes motifs from *c*
185–209 (25)	new material + ritornello	*a*	[A min–C maj]	violin demi-semiquavers; recorders and strings have motif *a*, followed by close canon
209–35 (27)	Ritornello 3	*a, d, e*	C maj	
235–63 (29)	Episode 3		C–G maj	
235–41 (7)	new material		[C maj]	solo and tutti violins in close canon
241–3 (3)	[ritornello]	*a*	[C maj]	
243–9 (7)			[C–G maj]	transposed variant of bars 119–25 from Episode 1

249–51 (3)	[ritornello]	*a*	[G maj]	
251–7 (7)			[G maj]	transposition of bars 235–41
257–63 (7)			[G–D maj]	transposition of bars 243–9
263–85 (22)	Ritornello 4	*c, b*	G maj	
285–323 (38)	Episode 4		G maj–B min	
285–311 (26)			[G maj–V of A]	transposed variant of bars 157–85 from Episode 2
311–23 (12)	[ritornello]	*c*	[V of A–B min]	
323–44 (22)	Ritornello 5	*a, d, e*	B min	
345–427 (83)	Ritornello 6	*a, b, c, d, e*	G maj	da capo repeat of bars 1–83

complete with opening and closing ritornellos, is repeated unchanged after a cadence in the mediant minor at bar 65.[18] None of the other Brandenburg movements is as straightforward as this, but elements of the da capo structure (particularly the iii–I tonal switch marking a return of the *Vordersatz*) impinge strongly on the first movements of Nos. 3 and 4 and both outer movements of No. 5. The third movement of No. 1 is a unique case of the so-called free da capo structure (see above, p. 48) translated into instrumental terms, and will be discussed in the next chapter.

If counterpoint is at a premium in Vivaldi's concertos, it may be said to be set at par in Bach's. This is particularly true of the Brandenburgs, of course, where the presence of more than one soloist (and usually of more than two) encourages imitation and permutation. Fugue is by no means unknown in Vivaldi's concertos, but it occurs rarely in the solo concertos that Bach is known to have been acquainted with by 1721, and in any case he had nothing to learn from the Italian master in this department of his art. It is perhaps only in the last movement of the Concerto for Two Harpsichords, BWV 1061, that Bach writes a concerto movement that might be called a fugue without qualification, but in other works the resources of fugue are often brought to bear in the construction of a ritornello or (less often) an episode. In the last movement of the

Fourth Brandenburg Concerto fugue and ritornello form are brought into closer amalgamation than they are in the first movement of the Concerto for Two Violins, BWV 1043, while the corresponding movement of No. 5 combines fugue with the da capo structure observed above. The nearest that Bach comes in the Brandenburg Concertos to writing a fugue is in the last movement of No. 2, which has many of the trappings of text-book fugue: a four-part exposition with regular counter-subject, middle entries in related keys, invertible counterpoint in the episodes, and so on. But even here there is one particular fugal episode (bars 48–57) which, by virtue of its distinctive material and its tutti instrumentation, is perceived as a kind of ritornello and serves (as in a normal ritornello movement) to reinforce the tonal centres of the movement.

Movements such as these provide ample evidence to show that Bach, in his melding of musical structures, as in his merging of genres, created no stereotypes.

6

The individual concertos

It is perhaps a measure of the richness and complexity of Bach's music that there is hardly a single major work by him which does not pose difficult, and often intractable, problems for the scholar – let alone the problems its poses for the interpreter. Even many of the smaller works can raise questions about authenticity, chronology, the priority of different versions, the intentions of the composer and so on, for which there may be as yet no certain answers, and the musicologist, like the performer, is frequently supplied with enough information to appreciate the complexity of a problem but insufficient information to resolve it. It would certainly ease the task of anyone studying the Brandenburg Concertos if the dedication copy were the sole surviving source.

The present chapter will be concerned mainly with what is in that dedication copy – the *Fassung letzter Hand* that Bach wrote out for the Margrave of Brandenburg in 1721 – but it will also touch on the pre-history of the individual concertos and on the way they were refashioned by Bach and, to some extent, by his later interpreters.

Concerto No. 1 in F major, BWV 1046

[Allegro] – Adagio – Allegro – Menuet

The first concerto is probably the oldest, in some of its parts at least, of all the Brandenburgs, and it is unique among all Bach's concertos in having four movements. These two observations are not necessarily connected, however; it is the circumstances, rather than the date, of its composition that seem to have influenced its final shape. It might appear at first glance that Bach has added an extra dance movement to the normal fast–slow–fast pattern of the Vivaldian concerto,[1] but in fact the genesis of the work is more complicated than that. The story of Bach's visit to Weissenfels in 1713, and of his composition there of the secular cantata *Was mir behagt, ist nur die muntre Jagd* (BWV 208) for the birthday of Duke Christian, has already been told (see above, pp. 11–14). The Sinfonia, BWV 1046*a* (formerly 1071), which is believed to have been composed as an introduction to this cantata, is extant in only one source, a score in the hand of Christian Friedrich Penzel, who had been a prefect at the Thomasschule, Leipzig, after Bach's death. It consists of the first, second and fourth movements of the First Brandenburg Concerto, but without the violino piccolo and without the polonaise in the last movement. Although dated April 1760, Penzel's copy transmits a version of these movements which pre-dates the 1721 score prepared for the Margrave of Brandenburg.[2]

It is not at all surprising that the editor Alfred Dörffel should have included the Sinfonia in F along with the four orchestral suites, BWV 1066–9, in volume 31/1 of the *BG*. As it stands in Penzel's score, the sinfonia does not much resemble a concerto, and its final minuet, especially, suggests strong links with the suite. The sinfonia does not, admittedly, begin with the measured Grave of a French overture, as do the four orchestral suites; nor is the opening fast movement a fugue. It is, nevertheless, close in style to the fugal movement of the C major orchestral suite, not least in the way the oboes either double the strings or detach themselves from them for short phrases only. The only movement suggestive of the Italian concerto style is the Adagio, in which the first oboe and first violin maintain a soloistic dialogue, with the bass instruments (bassoon and continuo) echoing their phrases in passages that define the tonal course of the music (G minor – A minor – D minor).

Bach clearly felt that these three movements, as they stood, were hardly suitable for a volume of concertos, and he therefore set about making the work more concerto-like by introducing an extra movement, placed third, with a solo part for the violino piccolo. Presumably he did this at some time between 1719 and 1721 with the margrave's commission in mind and, having decided upon it, he then revised the other movements so as to include the violino piccolo in them too, at the same time composing a polonaise as an additional 'trio' for the minuet. In December 1726 he found a new use for the added Allegro as the opening chorus of Cantata No. 207, *Vereinigte Zwietracht der wechselnden Saiten*, written for the inauguration of Gottlieb Kortte (1698–1731) as professor of jurisprudence at Leipzig University. In this D major chorus the voice parts (SATB) take over the material of the violino piccolo in the concerto.

Table 4 *Brandenburg Concerto No. 1: 3rd movement (Allegro)*

Bar nos. (total)	Ritornello/episode	Motifs	Keys	Remarks
A ('Exposition')				
1–17 (17)	Ritornello 1	*a, b, c, d*	F maj	for motifs see Ex. 11
1–4 (4)	*Vordersatz*	*a*		
5–7 (3)	*Fortspinnung I*	*b*		
8–11 (4)	*Fortspinnung II*	*c*		
12–17 (6)	*Epilog*	*d*		
17–40 (23)	Episode 1	*a, x*	F–C maj	frequent incursions of ritornello material
40–53 (13)	Ritornello 2	*b, c, d*	C maj	
B ('Middle section')				
53–63 (11)	Episode 2	new, *x*	C maj–A min	
63–70 (7)	Ritornello 3	*c, d*	A min	
70–83 (13)	Episode 3	new, *x*	A min–B♭ maj	includes passage in G min
A' ('Recapitulation')				
84–108 (25)	Episode 4	*a, x*	F maj	bars 84–91 = bars 17–24; bars 92–108 = bars 25–40, modified to remain in F
108–24 (17)	Ritornello 4	*a, b, c, d*	F maj	exact repeat of Ritornello 1

It was pointed out in the previous chapter that there are a number of instances in Bach's concertos where an episode modulating from tonic to dominant is later 'recapitulated' in such a way that it ends in the tonic, and it was suggested that this practice might be directly related to the so-called free da capo form found in many of the arias in the cantatas and other vocal works. But the Allegro of the First Brandenburg Concerto is the only instance in all Bach's concertos of a movement which adopts this structure in all its details, even to the restricting of new episodic material to what in an aria would be the middle (B) section. There are, on the other hand, a number of cantata choruses which employ the structure most successfully,[8] and the unprejudiced listener is likely to agree that the music at present under discussion sounds more at home in BWV 207 than it does in BWV 1046.

Ex. 11   Brandenburg Concerto No. 1, third movement

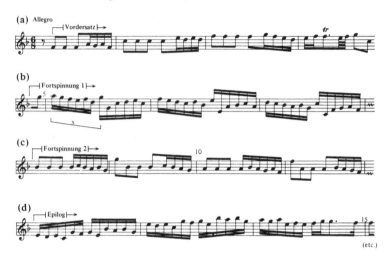

(etc.)

There is, of course, no reason why Bach should not have adapted the so-called free da capo structure to the concerto – he did, after all, use the strict da capo form for that purpose several times. The fact remains, however, that the Allegro of the First Brandenburg Concerto is exceptional in this respect, and in any case it is not only the overall structure that suggests a vocal origin for this movement. More revealing still are its internal proportions, for the relationship in length between the ritornellos and the episodes is altogether untypical of a concerto movement. Whereas the episodes seem mostly too short to allow the soloist room to shine, they are ideally proportioned to accommodate a clause of text in a vocal piece. The first episode in particular has all the hallmarks of a vocal movement. As was mentioned earlier (see p. 47), in an aria or chorus it is usually the initial text phrase that inspires the basic musical idea, and the normal practice is to employ this for the opening ritornello as well. As far as the listener is concerned it will seem that the vocal entry 'usually quotes from the opening ritornello. Sometimes just the opening motive, sometimes a whole phrase, and occasionally even the entire ritornello is sung.'[9] In a concerto movement, on the other hand, the normal practice is for the solo entry *not* to quote the ritornello opening. Occasionally it may begin with an ornamented version of it, but even this is comparatively rare. Perhaps the only instances in Bach's original concertos (including those he arranged for one or more harpsichords in Leipzig) are to be found in the first movement of the A minor Violin Concerto and the last movement of the Sixth Brandenburg Concerto; in both cases (especially the first) the solo version is considerably altered from that of the tutti. In the case of the movement under discussion, however, the violino piccolo begins its first solo by quoting the ritornello opening exactly, just as would normally occur in a vocal piece (Ex. 12; cf. Ex. 11a, above). Also significant in this context is the observation that it is not until the B section that the soloist contributes any new material – a feature which would be unremarkable in any vocal piece in da capo form.

There is, finally, the question of style. John Butt has identified the opening of the Gloria in Bach's B minor Mass as an example of 'a style

Ex. 12   Brandenburg Concerto No. 1, third movement

violino piccolo

derived from two similar dances, the Gigue and Passepied', with rhythms such as ♪♪♪ | ♪♪♪♪ particularly characteristic, and he suggests that this style 'was also important in final movements of concertos'.[10] The gigue/passepied rhythm, however, is only one element of the style; others include the major tonality and the confident, arpeggiaic thrust of the opening. It is precisely these features that characterize the third movement of the First Brandenburg Concerto, but there are no examples of such a movement in the other Brandenburgs, and the only one that comes close to it in any of Bach's other concertos is the last movement of the E major Harpsichord Concerto, BWV 1053, where the 3/8 time signature and the triplet semiquaver figuration suggest a somewhat slower tempo than that of a gigue.[11] As Butt mentions, the editor of the B minor Mass for the *NBA*, Friedrich Smend, went as far as to suggest that the 'Gloria in excelsis Deo' from that work was actually a concerto movement with vocal parts added. But the 'Hosanna in excelsis' (another parody) from the same work, the closing chorus of BWV 208 and the first and last choruses of both *Tönet, ihr Pauken*, BWV 214, and *Preise dein Glücke*, BWV 215, all serve to show that the style belongs more to the secular

n to the concerto, and we are therefore more likely to
ranslations from cantata to concerto in this style than the
reverse. This, I think, is what has happened in the case of the First
Brandenburg Concerto.

Evidence in support of the contrary and widely accepted view – that
the opening chorus of BWV 207 is adapted from the concerto movement
– might seem at first to be overwhelming. To begin with, the level of
corrections in the autograph of *Vereinigte Zwietracht der wechselnden
Saiten*[12] shows that we are dealing here with a composing score. If Bach
were merely parodying an existing chorus, even with a change of key and
perhaps of instrumentation, one might expect a cleaner, more fluently
written manuscript than P 174. Secondly, as Werner Neumann pointed
out,[13] it looks as though Bach, when he reached bar 58 in the cantata
chorus, began to copy the oboe part from BWV 1046 and then had to
alter it to fit the new passage that is inserted at that point (see Fig. 4).
Actually the obliteration is very heavy, and what originally lay beneath it
is to some extent conjectural, but Neumann's suggestion – that the
original oboe part was substantially the same as in the concerto at that
point – is a reasonable one. (This is not to say, however, that it was
copied from the concerto.)

Neumann and others have also pointed out that the irregular metre
and scansion of the chorus text suggest that it was written (probably by
Bach himself) to fit music that already existed. The versification is
certainly irregular:

> Vereinigte Zwietracht der wechselnden Saiten,
> Der rollenden Pauken durchdringender Knall!
> Locket den lüsteren Hörer herbei,
> Saget mit euren frohlockenden Tönen
> Und doppelt vermehretem Schall
> Denen mir emsig ergebenen Söhnen,
> Was hier der Lohn der Tugend sei.

[Resolved discords of quivering strings, penetrating sound of rolling kettledrums!
Draw hither the desirous listener, announce, with your jubilant tones and doubly
augmented sound, to my diligently dutiful sons what the reward for virtue might
be here.][14]

The fifth line seems to lack two or three syllables, but the scansion jars
most of all in the final line.[15] In fact, as far as the versification (but not

the sense) is concerned, the text would reach a satisfactory conclusion with 'Schall', and the lack of a rhyme between the final line and either of the first two is one of the most uncommon things about this chorus.[16]

To sum up, it would seem that the versification, the correction in the oboe part at bars 58–61 and the state of the autograph manuscript all support the orthodox view that Bach adapted the chorus from the concerto movement. But they do not prove conclusively that he did so. It should be noted that these three features are concentrated in the five bars (58–62) where the musical substance of the chorus first diverges from that of the concerto Allegro. It is there that the versification is fractured; it is there that the oboe part is reworked; and it is there that the autograph is most overladen with compositional second thoughts (see Fig. 4). The many corrections elsewhere are easily explicable as oversights in the process of adjusting the music to a new key and a different instrumental ensemble.

There seems to be only one explanation to account for all the puzzling and seemingly contradictory features of this movement: that Bach adapted both the concerto Allegro and the cantata chorus from a still earlier vocal composition. He would by 1721 have had quite a store of such works to choose from, since, as Friedrich Smend established, he was required to produce at least four new cantatas or similar works each year: two for 10 December (Prince Leopold's birthday) and two for New Year's Day.[17] The invitation to compose BWV 207 in Kortte's honour came from the Leipzig University students, who probably supplied Bach with the text to be set (as they did later in the case of the memorial service for the Electress Christiane Eberhardine, held in the university church in October 1727). Although Kortte's inauguration came during Advent, when cantatas were not required for the Sunday services in the main Leipzig churches, Bach quite probably found himself with little time to fulfil the commission and decided to re-use for the opening chorus a piece which he had already arranged for the First Brandenburg Concerto. Music and text did not fit each other exactly, but with some modifications they could be made to serve the purpose pretty well.

We may ask, then, what this lost original was like. Clearly it was a vocal piece, most probably an SATB chorus, judging from the violino piccolo's multiple stops in the Brandenburg version. Its text was probably of two-plus-four lines (rather than the two-plus-five of BWV 207) and at least the first line, and probably others, began with an anapaest (admittedly rare in the cantata literature). The most likely key for such a

Fig. 4 Cantata No. 207, first chorus, bars 55–64 (autograph); Berlin, Staatsbibliothek

Preußischer Kulturbesitz, Musikabteilung, Mus. ms. Bach P174

chorus would be D major, but it would appear from certain copying errors in BWV 207 that Bach was transposing it from F major.[18] If the chorus as we now know it were to be transposed up a minor third into F major it would require some reorganization of the middle voices in a few places, but the soprano part (except for a single top c''') would actually be enhanced by the change. In D major it lies rather low. On the other hand, the bass solo at the beginning of the chorus would then include an exposed, and perhaps unlikely, top f'.

There must be some complex explanation for all this: it might be, for example, that Bach did not have the original chorus to hand when he wrote BWV 207, and was forced to work from the Brandenburg recension. The simple explanation – that the movement really was originally composed for Brandenburg No. 1 – is scarcely believable.

We may now look a little more closely at the other three movements of the concerto. The ritornello structure of the first is clearly articulated, the rich panoply of sound in the tutti sections contrasting with the kaleidoscopic changes of texture as material is passed from horns to oboes, from oboes to violins. Much of the episodic material consists of semiquaver figures either derived from the ritornello itself or closely related to it, and this makes the movement particularly well-knit, even for Bach. The return in the tonic (at bars 63–72) of some episodic material first heard in the dominant (at bars 34–43) enhances the structural integrity of the movement. Compared with the sinfonia version, the autograph score shows several minor improvements to the part-writing and some rearrangement of the horn parts. There are few revisions of substance, but the F major inflexion in the harmonies of bars 7–8 and 78–9, replacing the move to D minor at similar points in the sinfonia, is a subtle reinforcement of the ritornello's tonal stability, and the change from tonic 6-4 to dominant chord on the fourth quaver strengthens the harmony of the first bar and is adopted in all subsequent appearances of the initial phrase. (Bach was rightly unconcerned about the fleeting 6-4 on the second semiquaver of the third beat in bar 10, but even this did not escape his attention on its return at bar 81 in the final ritornello!)

The Adagio recalls the slow movement of Bach's two-violin concerto, BWV 1043, in the way the two soloists (oboe and violino piccolo) unfold a stream of elaborately ornamented melody, at first separately but then in close imitation (and at times in canon). But whereas the Adagio of BWV 1043 is like a love duet, the Brandenburg's song is one of pain and suffering, at its most intense in the false-relation clashes between upper

Ex. 13 Brandenburg Concerto No. 1, second movement

and lower auxiliaries when the soloists relinquish the theme to the bass instruments at bars 9–11, 20–22 and 31–3. In the sinfonia version of this movement the dissonances thrown up by the compositional logic of these passages (as well as some of the semitonal clashes between the two soloists in bars 14 and 25) are smoothed away by means of chromatic or rhythmic alteration (Ex. 13). There is no reason, though, to suppose that all the discrepancies that exist between the two versions stem from Bach's own revisions. The alterations to the main theme when it is transferred to the bass must have been made with the sole purpose of mollifying the dissonances just mentioned, but it seems improbable that Bach was unwilling to tolerate in 1713 or 1716 a level of dissonance which he was to find acceptable in 1721. The false relations are much more likely to have offended Penzel's sensibilities in 1760.[19] Other revisions in the slow movement are of minor importance, but the substitution of the violin by the violino piccolo prompted Bach to place that instrument's first entry at a higher octave.

Among late Baroque conventions in both sonata and concerto was that of tacking a 'Phrygian' cadence on to the end of a slow movement in a minor key. After a normal perfect cadence in the tonic, the bass usually descends one tone to the flattened seventh, which is harmonized with a first-inversion minor triad; the bass then descends another tone and then a semitone, and these notes are harmonized with a minor triad in first inversion and a major triad in root position respectively to form the Phrygian cadence (IV^6–V).[20] The convention can be observed in several of the trio sonatas in Corelli's op. 1 (1683), where, however, the first chord of the link is usually omitted; in the composer's second set of *da chiesa* trio sonatas, op. 3 (1694), the chord on the flattened seventh is always included (see Ex. 14). The first two chords of the link lent themselves to embellishment, either improvised or written out (as in the Fourth Brandenburg Concerto), and occasionally the polyphonic fabric of the movement was continued through the link (as in the Sixth). In the first concerto Bach turns the convention into something disturbingly original. The expected conclusion of the movement at bar 36 is side-stepped by rests in the the upper parts, and then each bass step of the link (except the last) is harmonized twice, the conventional chords of the oboes being cancelled by unexpected harmonies in the strings which produce more of the false relations that have characterized the movement as a whole (Ex. 15). There is perhaps no parallel to this strangely beautiful succession of 'frozen' harmonies until we reach Stravinsky's *Dumbarton Oaks* (1938).[21]

Ex. 14   Corelli, Sonata op. 3 no. 4, third movement

Ex. 15   Brandenburg Concerto No. 1, second movement

If the progression from this highly individual Phrygian cadence to the opening of the F major Allegro sounds discontinuous to modern ears, the beginning of the Menuet, with its foreign E♭, might have surprised even Bach's audience for the sinfonia. This is another unusual movement (especially for a concerto): a minuet, originally with two trios, to which Bach added a polonaise followed by an additional return of the minuet. The minuet itself is thus heard between four and eight times in all (depending on how many times the repeats are observed), and the purpose of the trios seems to be to introduce as much variety as possible within this repetitive framework. The first, in D minor, uses the quintessentially French, specifically Lullyan, combination of two oboes and bassoon. The 'Poloinesse', as Bach called it, is in F major and 3/8 metre, and is scored for strings alone without violino piccolo, which could not have played the low notes in bar 29. The polonaise may be thought of as an episode within a rondo structure, allowing the strings a soloistic role to balance those of the woodwind in Trio 1 and the horns in Trio 2. Why Bach should have chosen a polonaise for this function is not at all clear; the Margrave of Brandenburg seems not to have had any particular involvement in Polish affairs. The possibility that it was done for a performance in Dresden, where the Elector Friedrich August I was also King of Poland, cannot be ruled out (Bach's connexions with the Saxon capital date from 1717, if not earlier). It is, at all events, a most unusual polonaise. The agogic accents on the second quaver of bars 4, 5, 6, 12 and 20 and the feminine cadence at the end of each phrase are perhaps the features most typical of the traditional dance, but the drone bass, particularly in the first half, is more suggestive of the musette. Two other unusual features are the initial upbeat (not at all typical of the polonaise and not present in Bach's other examples of it)[22] and the sudden intrusion of a detached, emphatic *forte* passage (bars 25–8) into the suave, legato *piano* expression of the rest of the piece. One senses a special significance in this movement without being able to identify what it is.

The second trio, again in F major but with a change of metre to 2/4, features the two horns as soloists; it is actually labelled 'Trio pour les Cors de chasse' in the sinfonia version, where the horns are accompanied by first and second violins in unison. Perhaps for greater variety (the strings having had the polonaise to themselves), Bach replaced the violins with unison oboes in the concerto; his revisions go beyond the necessary avoidance of the b♭s in bar 23, which lie outside the compass of the oboe, but the result is clearly a simplified and tidied-up version of the earlier part and not a newly composed one. When he came to use the music again, as a final ritornello for the duet 'Den soll mein Lorbeer schützend decken' in Cantata No. 207, he retained the concerto version, merely transcribing it in D major for two trumpets and unison oboes d'amore and *taille* (tenor oboe) and adding light accompanying chords for the strings in the last four bars of each section.

The complex origins of the First Brandenburg Concerto are further complicated by one final observation concerning this movement. In

Penzel's score the third oboe doubles the viola, whose part descends as far as f. It is therefore evident that the ensemble for which Bach wrote the original version of the minuet included as its woodwind component the standard combination of two oboes, tenor oboe and bassoon.[23] Not surprisingly, when he came to transfer the minuet to the concerto he was obliged to rewrite those passages for the third oboe (no longer a *taille*) which lay outside its compass. What is perhaps surprising is that the first movement of the sinfonia also contains a number of passages in which, while the first and second oboes double the first and second violins exactly, the third oboe doubles the viola only as long as the part does not go below c', the oboe's lowest note.[24] This suggests (though it does not actually prove) that the first movement, and probably the second, of the sinfonia (and therefore of the concerto as well) originated separately from the minuet.

In 1726 Bach re-used the first movement of the First Brandenburg Concerto as an introductory sinfonia to the cantata *Falsche Welt, dir trau ich nicht* (BWV 52), performed on the twenty-third Sunday after Trinity (24 November). He did not include the violino piccolo on this occasion, but in most other important respects (for example in the harmony of bar 1 and similar contexts, and in the horn parts of bars 69–71) the cantata version follows that of Brandenburg No. 1. It is interesting to note, however, that the cantata version also resurrects certain details of the earlier sinfonia, BWV 1046*a*: the horns revert to their original roles in bars 8–12, for example, and the modulation to D minor is reinstated in bars 7–8 and 78–9. There are also a number of places where the cantata version differs from both the earlier ones; one of these is bar 33, where the horns' $b\natural$'s become $b\flat$'s.[25] Clearly, Bach continued to revise and polish the music even after its inclusion in the presentation score.

Bach's re-use of the third movement of the First Brandenburg Concerto (or whatever piece that movement was based on) in Cantata No. 207 (1726) has already been described in some detail. For the sake of completeness, it should be mentioned here that he used the same music again, probably in 1735, as the opening chorus of the cantata *Auf, schmetternde Töne der muntern Trompeten* (BWV 207*a*) for the name-day of the Elector Friedrich August II.

Concerto No. 2 in F major, BWV 1047

[Allegro] – Andante – Allegro assai

Whereas the first of the Brandenburg Concertos brings together movements evidently written at different times and for different purposes, the second concerto shows no signs of similar heterogeneous origins in its make-up. There are no reasons for supposing it to have been conceived as anything other than a concerto or for believing that its three movements did not always belong together, despite the different levels of orchestral participation from one movement to the next.

The opening movement, however, leaves far behind the straight-forward ritornello form of the Italians. It is, in fact, one of the most complex structures in all Bach's concertos. The main tonal outlines, are, as usual, clear enough, with well-articulated 'rhyming' cadences embracing all the keys most nearly related to that of the movement as a whole: F major (bar 8), C major (28), D minor (39), B♭ major (59), G minor (83), A minor (102) and again F major at the end (118). But there is no regular alternation of solo and tutti throughout the movement, and without these cadential landmarks it would be very difficult for the listener to find an aural path through an extremely varied musical terrain, which is coloured by practically every possible combination of the instruments used, from the simple violin and continuo of the first episode (bars 9–10) to such densely-textured passages as bars 77–81, in which nearly every line is thematic (Ex. 16). While it is possible to identify bars 1–8 as constituting an opening ritornello, the episode that follows (bars 9–22) is broken up by two-bar tutti restatements of the opening ritornello motif and, after another brief tutti (bars 23–8), the participation of the *ripieno* instruments is so thorough-going that it becomes no longer profitable to attempt an analysis in terms of ritornello–episode or tutti–solo. Alberto Basso's division of the movement into two equal sections of 59 bars each has something to commend it, especially as the material and texture of the first episode are recalled at the beginning of his second section;[26] but Elke Lang-Becker is surely right to see practically the whole of the movement, from bar 28 to bar 102, as development ('Durchführung'), though one might argue with her about where each of the 'first and second developments' begins.[27] A weakness of Basso's bipartite division is that it fails to recognize the iii–I conjunction at bars 102–3, together with the unison restatement of the opening motif that follows, as a structural

Ex. 16 Brandenburg Concerto No. 2, first movement

'event'; and Lang-Becker's use of analytical terminology borrowed from Classical sonata structures is not perhaps entirely appropriate, either, to the movement as a whole. The fact is that this music follows no blueprint, and to attempt an analysis that goes beyond its tonal structure would be to account for every bar – in other words, to reproduce the entire score. Even the final ritornello, which in most movements of this kind is no more than a routine repeat of the opening tutti, brings an element of surprise when a half-forgotten passage from earlier in the movement (bars 50–55) is interpolated at bars 107–12, with its last bass note sharpened to accommodate a diminished seventh on B♮, thereby strengthening the return to F major at the end.[28]

Following a tradition imposed on the concerto by the technical limitations of the valveless instrument, if not by its timbre, Bach does not include the trumpet in the Andante. In fact, the movement is scored as a piece of chamber music for the other three solo instruments and basso continuo only. The thematic structure is even more economical than that of the first movement, the whole of the material being contained in the violin's opening two-bar motif and the counterpoint it plays to the oboe's repetition of it (Ex. 17). Various combinations of these motifs are deployed between the soloists above a bass whose continuous, purposeful quaver movement is broken only at the cadences that define the tonal course of the music: A minor (bars 14–15), C major (22–3), B♭ major (32–3), G minor (42–3) and the tonic (D minor) at the end.

Ex. 17   Brandenburg Concerto No. 2, second movement

The violin has until this point acted as *primus inter pares* among the four solo instruments. Not only has it been the first to lead off as soloist in each movement, it has also imposed its character on the style of the music, sometimes to the discomfort of the other instruments. The Allegro assai, however, belongs principally to the trumpet. It is the trumpet that announces the main theme, a fugue subject obviously styled to suit the instrument. Although often described as an amalgam of fugue and ritornello typical of the composer, the movement's structure is quite unlike the combinations of fugue and ritornello found in the finales of the fourth and fifth concertos, or in the first movement of the Concerto for Two Violins, BWV 1043. It is, in fact, much more of a fugue and much less of a ritornello movement than they are. It opens with a formal exposition consisting of subject (trumpet), answer (oboe), subject (violin) and answer (recorder); there is a regular counter-subject, and the trumpet even makes a brave attempt at a redundant entry of the answer (despite not having the required E♮ in its vocabulary); middle entries occur in C major (violin, bar 57), D minor (oboe, bar 66), the dominant of D minor (bass, bar 72) and B♭ major (oboe, bar 107), and final entries in F major (recorder, bar 113) and its dominant (bass, bar 119), and the trumpet, appropriately enough, rounds off the movement with a final recall of the first part of the subject. The *ripieno* strings are not heard at all until bar 47, and it is only because they add light harmonic support to the cadential approaches that we perceive any ritornello element at all. As in the case of the last (fugal) movement of the Concerto for Two Harpsichords, BWV 1061, the orchestral strings (though not, of course, in this case the basso continuo) could be omitted without any real loss to the fabric of the music.

Concerto No. 3 in G major, BWV 1048

[Allegro] – Adagio – Allegro

The third concerto is generally thought to be among the earliest of all the Brandenburgs, at least as far as its first movement is concerned. Martin Geck saw it as a high point in the German tradition of the ensemble sonata, or Ouverture, often used as an introduction to a church cantata, and proposed a composition date before 1714, in other words before Italian influence began to impinge strongly on Bach's instrumental music.[29] He found some impressive evidence to support this in the version of the first movement used as an introduction to Cantata No. 174 (1729; see below). Two of the copyists employed in preparing the score and parts for this cantata (and in one case even Bach himself) had cancelled sharp signs with flats (♭) instead of naturals (♮), an old-fashioned practice which Bach himself abandoned in 1715.[30] There are, however, certain stylistic features in the music, particularly its motor-rhythms and unison passages, that might suggest a period of composition when the influence of Vivaldi on Bach's work was already quite strong. Also, the disposition of solo and tutti, as well as the organization of the musical material itself, is so complex, original and masterful that one must wonder whether Bach would or could have written a movement like this as early as Geck suggested.

Hans-Joachim Schulze resolved this conflict between style and chronology by postulating the existence of an intermediate fair copy of the concerto made by someone in the Bach circle who indiscriminately used both ♭ and ♮ signs to cancel sharps.[31] These accidentals, he suggested, were then taken over by the team of copyists who worked on the material for Cantata No. 174 in 1729. Schulze even proposed a likely candidate as copyist of the intermediate score: a scribe from the Cöthen circle (perhaps Emanuel Lebrecht Gottschalck) whose instrumental parts for a 1720 performance in Hamburg of Bach's Cantata No. 21 exhibit the same notational mannerism. Gottschalck (*d.* 1727) was employed at the Cöthen court from 1714 as *Kammerdiener*, and from 1719 as copyist: in that year he assisted Bach in bringing the new Mietke harpsichord from Berlin.

The Third Brandenburg Concerto is scored for three each of violins, violas and cellos, supported by violone (of the 'grosso' type) and harpsichord. The basic tutti disposition is defined by the opening eight-bar ritornello, in which the instruments of each type play in unison, the cellos also being in unison with the continuo bass, making a sonorous three-part texture. The scoring of the episodes is extremely varied; there may be antiphony between different groups playing the same motif (as in bars 9–10 and 16–17, for example), or the three groups might combine and exchange different motifs (as in bars 32–8), or yet again a single instrument may detach itself from the rest for a brief solo (as the first and second violins do, for instance, in bars 47–54). As in the corresponding movement of the second concerto, the surface of the music is constantly changing, but here within a basic monochrome and resting on a solid structural framework.

The framework in this case is basically tripartite (ABA'), the first section ending with a reprise of the opening ritornello in G major at bars 39–46. An unusual feature of this return is that the music, although fundamentally the same as in bars 1–8, is completely rescored. The first violin part is transferred to a higher octave, and in place of the original three-strand texture we have at times divided violins and violas, thus increasing the sonority of what was already a richly resonant string sound. At the beginning of the middle section (bar 47) the *doh'–te–doh'* motif (see above, p. 42), which permeates this movement more than any other in the set, gives rise to a new figure in the first violin which is then passed to the second and later (bar 67) to the third. For the rest, this middle section is content to review earlier material, ending at bar 77 with a cadence in the mediant (B) minor. This cadence naturally prompts expectations of a repeat of the first section in the manner of a da capo aria; but although the final section does indeed begin in G and ends with a complete restatement of the opening ritornello in that key (and in its original scoring), it is far from being the literal repeat of the first section that convention demands. It cannot, in fact, be described as anything less than a full-scale second development of all the themes and motifs so far heard. It begins not with a new counterpoint to the main ritornello theme, as is sometimes stated, but with a conflation of the violin and viola figures from bars 1–2 in the manner of a double fugue (subject, bars 78–9; answer, bars 80–81; subject (violas), bars 86–7), and continues to develop both ritornello and episodic material at length and in keys (including A minor and G minor) not hitherto visited. Its length exceeds that of the first section by about the same amount as the first section exceeds the second.

This unusually proportioned, tightly organized and immensely enjoyable movement is followed by another which is no less remarkable, but in a very different way. The Adagio consists of a time signature (C) and two minim chords only – those needed to form the conventional Phrygian cadence at the end of a slow movement in E minor. These two chords raise a number of questions, and a great deal of ink has been spilled in attempts to answer them. Has a leaf been lost from the presentation copy? Did Bach simply omit a movement when he came to write out the fair copy for the margrave? Did he intend the two chords to stand alone as a slow movement? Did he require another solo movement to be inserted at that point? Did he envisage a solo improvisation instead? What, in short, would Prince Leopold have heard in a performance under Bach at Cöthen?

The first two questions are easily answered. There is no possibility that a movement has been lost from the presentation copy, since the two chords stand in the middle of a page, where they separate the end of the first movement from the beginning of the Allegro (see Fig. 3). In Penzel's score, made from an earlier version after Bach's death, they follow immediately on the end of the first movement at the bottom of a page, and they appear in similar fashion in the parts copied from that score in 1755.[32] Attempts to answers the other questions invariably raise further questions in their wake. If we decide to insert a complete movement at this point, which Adagio in E minor, common time, should it be, and why did Bach not enter such a movement in the score? Are we justified in inserting a solo movement when the Phrygian cadence itself is fully scored? If, instead, we substitute an improvisation, on what instrument should it be played? Should it precede the two chords, or separate them, or both? And why, then, did Bach specify an Adagio tempo?

Against the unanswerable question as to what Leopold's ensemble at Cöthen would have played at this point, we may place a still more intriguing question: how would the Margrave of Brandenburg's ensemble have dealt with the problem? Without Bach himself to guide them, they would surely have been placed in a novel situation, since they could never have encountered in printed concertos (and the presentation copy has all the finish and authority of a print) a work in which the composer abdicated responsibility for an entire movement. English musicians, it is true, had later to adapt themselves to a similar situation when playing some of Handel's organ concertos, but not in works printed under the composer's supervision and without so much as an 'ad lib' direction. They at least knew that an improvisation was called for, and which player was expected to supply it.

The ways in which performers have dealt with the problem have been many and varied; several of them are mentioned by Norman Carrell.[33] Some conductors (though not many nowadays) solemnly play the two chords unadorned, just as they stand in the score. Others insert a movement from another Bach work, the third movement of the G major Violin Sonata, BWV 1021, and the second of the G major Organ Sonata, BWV 530, being among those most favoured. As Emil Platen pointed out, one can at least invoke a Bachian precedent for this procedure, since Bach himself drew on the slow movement of his Organ Sonata in D minor, BWV 527, for the middle movement of the Triple Concerto in A minor, BWV 1044.[34] (He did not, however, 'borrow' a movement he had not yet written!) A solution more often adopted is to precede the two chords with an improvisatory few bars on a chord progression such as that which Handel provided for the *ad libitum* fourth movement of his Organ Concerto in A major, HWV 296a. The difficulty here is to decide which instrument should do the 'improvising'. To choose the harpsichord, as is frequently done, is to elevate it to a rank of importance which it does not enjoy in the rest of the work; the first violin or the first viola (which Bach himself might well have played in Cöthen performances, if there were any) is perhaps a better choice, but might seem to need some continuo support. Platen devised a quasi-improvisatory 'Gruppenkadenz', thirteen bars long, which employed the complete ensemble, but this does not seem to have been widely adopted, either as a solution or as a blueprint for one.[35] Perhaps the best course of all is to acknowledge that we can never know for certain what Bach himself would have done and to dodge the problem altogether by going straight from the end of the first movement to the beginning of the Allegro. The two fast movements are, after all, quite well contrasted.

The Allegro is another exceptional movement. Except for the Sinfonia that opens the second part of Cantata No. 35 and which probably started life as the last movement of a concerto for violin or oboe, it is the only concerto movement by Bach to use the binary dance form of two sections, each marked for repeat. This is a structure which Vivaldi used not infrequently in the final movements of concertos, but one which Bach otherwise reserved for suites and, occasionally, sonatas. Bach's movement is in the style of a gigue and exhibits the regular phrase-lengths of a dance, but is somewhat unusual in its proportions, the second section being three times as long as the first. This is accounted for by the fact that the binary structure encompasses both a ternary and a ritornello design; the subdivisions are clearly articulated by cadential patterns but at the same time smoothed over by the homogeneity of the semiquaver figuration, from which the first violin motif at bars 15–16 (recalled by the first viola at bars 35–6), with its tripping demisemiquavers, stands out as a thematic 'event'. The movement's structure may be summarized thus:

Sections	‖ : A —	: ‖	: B —	A'—	B'—	A"—	: ‖
Keys	: G—D	: ‖	: D — e	e — b	b — C	C—G	: ‖
Bar nos.	: 1—12	: ‖	: 13—16	17—28	29—36	37—48	: ‖

Except for the seventh note in the bass at bar 39 and some interchange of material between the violins and violas, the final section (A", bars 37–48) constitutes an exact subdominant recapitulation of the first (bars 1–12).

Another feature of the Allegro, in contrast with the first movement, is that the three cellos and the violone play in unison throughout, although Bach in his presentation score continued to allot a separate staff to each instrument. Taken together with the 'missing' Adagio and the unusual structure of the finale, this observation makes it difficult to ignore the possibility that the movements of the Third Brandenburg Concerto, like those of the first, originally existed separately and may have been brought together in fulfilment of the margrave's commission.

Bach returned to the first movement of the Third Brandenburg Concerto for the sinfonia that opens the cantata *Ich liebe den Höchsten von ganzem Gemüte* (No. 174), composed for the second day of Whitsun (6 June) 1729. For this he retained virtually unaltered the original violin, viola and cello parts (though with even fewer *divisi* passages for the three cellos than in the Brandenburg version), re-cast portions of the continuo part,[36] which he also reinforced with a bassoon, and added new parts for two horns (*corni da caccia*) two oboes and *taille* (the woodwind instruments being doubled by *ripieno* violins and viola). Bach distinguishes the original violin, viola and cello parts with the designation 'concertato' (or, for the violas, 'concertata') but, curiously enough, the added instruments are not used to sharpen the distinction between ritornello and episode in the movement. Quite the reverse, in fact. They are silent for only nine bars (78–86) in all, and achieve a fair measure of independence. They serve, in fact, to disguise the concerto origins of the movement – or perhaps to emphasize its origins outside the concerto! Another surprise, perhaps, is that Bach is quite ready to sacrifice most of the octave scale passages that originally underlined climactic points in the music (for example, at bar 125).

Concerto No. 4 in G major, BWV 1049

Allegro – Andante – Presto

The fourth concerto is one of the most substantial in the whole set, and the only one in which the entire forces are employed in all the movements. Its opening Allegro nevertheless achieves a lightness of texture which derives partly from its dance-like rhythms in 3/8 metre, partly from the choice of violin and two recorders for the solo group and partly from the light orchestral accompaniment in the episodes. The movement was analysed in some detail in chapter 5 (see pp. 52–7), where the dual nature of the opening section (bars 1–83), which functions as both ritornello and the first section of a da capo structure, was also commented on. As was shown there, the restatements of the ritornello in E minor (bar 137), C major (209) and B minor (323) are considerably foreshortened, each one recalling only the *Vordersatz*, the third *Fortspinnung* and the *Epilog* of the original ritornello (i.e. Ex. 9, a, d and e).

There are also several references to ritornello material during the episodes, including a complete return of the second *Fortspinnung* (bars 35–57) at bars 263–85. The independent participation of the three soloists in the opening ritornello practically ensures that the episodic material will have its own distinctive physiognomy, and the contrast is at its sharpest in the second episode when the solo violin takes flight in a scale passage of dazzling demisemiquavers (bars 187–209). Such passages as this, together with similar ones in the last movement, have encouraged commentators to look upon the work as essentially a violin concerto, but in fact the recorders (always as a pair) are given a fair share of soloistic prominence, and it is their section of the second episode (bars 157–85) that Bach recalls later in the movement, with extra string participation (bars 285–311).

If the violin tends to outshine the recorders in virtuosity in the outer movements, it is allotted a decidedly subservient role in the Andante, where (except for a single bar) its function is to provide a bass for the wind instruments, when it is not merely doubling the orchestral violins.[37] The movement, based largely on its lilting opening figure, takes the form:

Sections	A	B	C	B'	C'
Keys	e	e — a	a — b	b — e	e
Bar nos.	1—18	19—28	29—45	46—55	56—67

in which B' is a transposed repeat of B, and C' a varied repeat of C. The movement ends with a Phrygian cadence decorated by the first recorder (not by the violin!).

The Presto, for all its high spirits, is probably the tightest and most satisfying convergence of ritornello form and fugue in all Bach's music. Unlike the first movement of the Concerto for Two Violins, BWV 1043, in which the fugue subject (except for its initial phrase) is heard only in the ritornello sections, or the last movement of the second Brandenburg, in which a kind of ritornello structure is imposed on a fugue by means of the instrumentation (see above, p. 78), this Presto constitutes a genuine and successful attempt to achieve a fusion, rather than merely an amalgam, of two radically different (one might even say opposed) structures. Since contrapuntal rigour and virtuoso display are not readily compatible with each other, compromises have to be made. The passage of dazzling scales and *bariolage* with which the solo violin reasserts its virtuoso hold on the concerto at bars 101–35 represents the major concession to ritornello form (although even here the fugue subject makes a shadowy appearance in the *ripieno* violins); the fact that the progress from one tonal centre to the next is effected more in the ritornello sections themselves than in the episodes may be understood as a concession to fugal propriety, as also perhaps should the tonic pedal that ushers in the remarkable coda – remarkable, that is, for the way the rhythm of the initial phrase of the fugue subject is expressed in imposing and repetitious homophony, with the accent thrown on to the second of the two minims (now staccato). The unexpected and climactic diminished seventh chord at bar 233 finds release in a final stretto statement of the subject by the basses and recorders.

This Presto is one of the few concerto finales by Bach not in one of the triple or compound metres strongly associated with dance music. Its *alla breve* time signature, its fugal texture and its length (244 bars) all contribute to shifting the 'weight' of the composition from the first to the last movement, and this is in strong contrast to the generality of late Baroque concertos by Bach's contemporaries (or, for that matter, by Bach himself). If the composer ever felt himself confronted by what in the nineteenth century became the 'finale problem' (and there is no reason to suppose he ever did), he solved it in the combination of *gravitas* and high spirits that characterizes the last movement of the Fourth Brandenburg Concerto.

In the 1730s or early 1740s Bach made a version of this concerto for harpsichord, two recorders and strings (BWV 1057), almost certainly for performance at the meetings of the collegium musicum which he directed at Gottfried Zimmermann's premises in Leipzig from 1729 to 1737, and again from 1739 to 1741 or later. It exists in an autograph manuscript containing seven such concerto arrangements (BWV 1052–8), together with a fragmentary eighth (BWV 1059), now in the Deutsche Staatsbibliothek, Berlin. Like most of the arrangements that Bach made from violin concertos, BWV 1057 has been transposed down one tone, into F major. If the reason for this was to bring the upper reaches of the solo violin part within the range of Bach's harpsichord (the treble of which extended to d'''), then he went to considerable trouble in this case to avoid a single note (the e''' in bar 194 of the first movement), since the only other note unobtainable on the harpsichord, the g''' in bar 63 of the ritornello (repeated at bar 407), remains unobtainable as f'''. Nowhere else in the first movement, and nowhere at all in the other two, does the solo violin reach beyond the d''' obtainable in unextended third position on the

E string. A more cogent reason for the downwards transposition in this case may have been to have the recorders play in a key which suited them better than G major does.

The transposition necessitates minor adjustments to the string and recorder parts but, as usual, Bach makes no alterations to the actual substance of the music; not a bar is added or subtracted. The balance of solo and tutti in the arrangement is, however, radically different from what it was in the original version. Bach writes new harpsichord counterpoints to the recorders' dialogues in bars 165–85 in the first movement (substantially repeated at bars 293–311) and bars 159–75 in the last movement; he enlivens the keyboard figuration with rapid passing notes in several places; and in the slow movement the harpsichord takes over the material originally allotted to all three soloists (including the first recorder's decoration of the Phrygian cadence). The result of all these revisions is to make BWV 1057 much more of a solo harpsichord concerto than BWV 1049 was a solo violin concerto.

Concerto No. 5 in D major, BWV 1050

Allegro – Affettuoso – Allegro

The Fifth Brandenburg Concerto occupies a special position in the history of the genre. Here, for the first time in a concerto, the harpsichord is elevated from the rank of continuo instrument to that of soloist. It would be inaccurate and misleading to call it a harpsichord concerto *tout court* – though the long and elaborate cadenza in the first movement underlines Bach's obvious intention to promote the harpsichord to a position of importance above that of the other soloists, violin and flute – and it may be that the harpsichord concertos Bach later wrote (or arranged) for the collegium musicum in Leipzig exerted a greater influence on the development of the new genre. But the number of extant sources of Brandenburg No. 5 far exceeds that of any of the others in the set,[38] and bears witness to the impression that this work must have made on Bach's contemporaries and immediate successors.

The concerto exists in three versions. The earliest is conveyed in a set of parts copied some time between 1744 and 1759 by Bach's pupil, assistant and son-in-law, Johann Christoph Altnikol,[39] helped by three other scribes; these parts, now in the Staatsbibliothek Preußischer Kultur- besitz, Berlin (St 132), can be shown to derive from a score earlier than

than the presentation autograph. Disregarding nineteenth-century amendments in the hand of Mendelssohn's teacher, Carl Friedrich Zelter, they differ from the later and familiar version in four major respects: as mentioned earlier, the cadenza in the first movement is only eighteen bars long (compared with sixty-five in the later version); the second movement is marked 'Adagio' (in the later version 'Affettuoso'); the passage at bars 177–82 in the third movement is replaced by one four bars longer in the later version; and there is no cello part.[40]

That these parts transmit a version earlier than that of the presentation score (although they were copied more than twenty years later) can be shown from a number of readings in them which appear again, but with corrections, in a set of autograph parts in the Deutsche Staatsbibliothek, Berlin (St 130). The autograph parts represent a second version of the concerto which includes the more extended cadenza in the first movement, and it was evidently from these (and perhaps also from another score, now lost) that Bach prepared the now familiar version of the concerto for the Margrave of Brandenburg, making as he did so a number of further revisions, including the expansion of bars 177–82 in the third movement.

The opening Allegro is the longest and most complex of all the Brandenburg movements, and yet it begins with the shortest of ritornellos, a mere eight bars of busy, almost unbroken semiquavers in the violins, supported by purposeful quavers in the lower strings. Although this ritornello exhibits the three sections (*Vordersatz*, bars 1–2; *Fortspinnung*, 3–7; and *Epilog*, 7–8) of Fischer's archetype (see page 48), the *Fortspinnung* here is not merely sequential, and what repetition it contains is subtly disguised by changes of metrical accent (see Ex. 18).

As might be expected, the first episode (bars 9–19) introduces a new idea – descending stepwise quavers encompassing a fourth (flute and violin), answered after a half close by the same figure inverted and decorated with semiquaver triplets – but the essential material for the rest of this first section is now complete. Alternation of ritornello and episode remains as the basis of the structure, but the concern for continuity and dynamic growth is something new. The return of the ritornello in A major (bar 19), for example, is interrupted by episodic development of the *Fortspinnung* material (bars 21–9, flute and violin), and the *Fortspinnung* itself (bars 29–31) is then followed by episodic development of the *Epilog* (bars 31–5, harpsichord) leading to a cadence in B minor. Beginning in that key, a conflation of the first two episodes (bars 42–58)

Ex. 18   Brandenburg Concerto No. 5, first movement

brings the harpsichord its first opportunity for virtuoso display in demisemiquaver scales, and this might seem to signal the approaching end of the opening section. Anticipation is sharpened by a tutti return of the ritornello *Fortspinnung* in D major (!) at bar 58, but the expected cadence is side-stepped when the flute takes up and develops the *Epilog* motif (bar 61) as a new counterpoint for the *Fortspinnung* motif (*x*) in a fresh episode that leads the music into F♯ minor and the start of the middle section.

The continuous growth and development that has characterized the movement up to this point is remarkable, but no less forward-looking is the relaxed central section (bars 71–101), which Bach clearly sees as something more than merely another episode and marks *pianissimo* throughout. Here the harmonic rhythm is slowed down to one chord per bar, while thematic activity is reduced to the repetition on flute and violin of a brief motif bearing a shadowy relationship to figure *x* from the ritornello (bars 71–80) and after that disappears altogether as the right hand of the keyboard part maintains an unchanging semiquaver figure against descending arpeggios played by the left hand and the other soloists in regular two-bar periods. All these features seem to point forward to the middle sections of several of Mozart's mature piano concertos (often labelled as 'development', but aptly described by Denis Forman as 'free fantasy'),[41] as also does the dominant (E) pedal that ushers in the return of the ritornello in A major at bar 101. The true recapitulation does not come until bar 110, however (giving the chance for development of yet another ritornello motif (*y*) at bars 103–4), when the first episode returns, with flute and violin exchanging roles and the course of the music altered so as to remain in D major. The ritornello that follows (bar 121) could easily have signalled the ending of the movement (just as it seemed to promise the end of the first section at bar 58), but Bach again side-steps the *Epilog* in favour of further recapitulation of previous material, as he does yet again at bar 139, where a passage of demisemiquaver scales recalling (and indeed incorporating) that at bars 47–9[42] leads straight into the cadenza.

Objections have been raised to the use of the term 'cadenza' for the long solo passage that Bach writes at this point. There is no pause mark in the score (a conventional sign for the introduction of bravura embellishment in both vocal and instrumental music), the passage does not decorate a cadence and Bach merely writes 'solo senza stromenti' against the cembalo part in the score. Moreover, in the earlier version the passage is more obviously a continuation of the demisemiquaver figuration begun at bar 139 and now prolonged, without thematic reference to the rest of the movement, to form a climactic lead-in to the final ritornello (which repeats the first *in toto*).[43] In the presentation score Bach makes the beginning of the solo more of an 'event' by halting the demisemiquaver figuration and inserting a new, 43-bar passage which brings fresh developments of both the first episode material and the right-hand figuration from the movement's middle section. The original bravura material is then resumed, but it is again slowed down, first to triplets and then to semiquavers, so that the cadenza may end, as it began, with thematic material.

Christoph Wolff conjectured, from the layout of the autograph score (see p. 39 and Fig. 2), that this longer form of the cadenza was not decided on until Bach came to write out the dedication copy.[44] According to Wolff, Bach appears to have made the reasonable estimate that the harpsichord solo, as originally composed, would require six pages of score; the solo part would occupy the two broader staves at the foot of each page and the other staves would be filled with rests. He prepared the manuscript paper accordingly. Having then decided upon a longer cadenza, he saw that it would require at least double the number of pages to accommodate it – an extravagance he could not contemplate. He therefore filled the staves already drawn with both the cadenza and the whole of the slow movement, abandoning the distinction between the harpsichord staves and those for the other instruments that he had carefully observed up to that point in the work.

It was suggested earlier (see p. 16) that the harpsichord cadenza may have been extended to unprecedented lengths in order to show the paces of the new instrument from Berlin, but Bach's over-riding concern seems to have been to integrate it into the fabric of the movement. That he thought of it as a cadenza (even if he would not have used the term himself) cannot be doubted. He was well aware of precedents for it in the concertos of Vivaldi (including the so-called *Grosso Mogul*, RV 208, which Bach arranged for organ, complete with its two elaborate cadenzas, as BWV 594) and no doubt those of other composers too. According to the flautist and theorist J. J. Quantz, solo cadenzas without accompaniment began to be used in the second decade of the eighteenth century:

between 1710 and 1716, or thereabouts, the cadenzas customary at present, in which the bass must pause, became the mode. Fermatas, in which one pauses *ad libitum* in the middle of a piece, may well have a somewhat earlier origin.[45]

What makes the cadenza of the Fifth Brandenburg Concerto so exceptional (perhaps unique) is its prophetic combination of thematic reference and brilliant passage-work in an improvisatory style.

The clearly articulated ritornello structure of the slow movement was described in some detail in the previous chapter (see pp. 52–3). Its tempo marking, Affettuoso, invites comment, if only because of its rarity in Bach's scores: Robert Marshall mentions only Cantata No. 71 (libretto) and the third movement of the not fully authenticated Violin Sonata in C minor, BWV 1024, as instances of its use outside Brandenburg No.5.[46] As mentioned above, the earliest version of this movement is marked 'Adagio'; possibly the change to 'Affettuoso' is connected with the 'affective' slurring that Bach added to many passages in the final version.

In the last movement of the Second Brandenburg Concerto Bach superimposed a ritornello design on a fugue; in the last movement of the fourth he achieved a close fusion of the two forms. Now he combines them with a third structure, that of the da capo aria. As in the second concerto, the four-part fugal exposition is played by the soloists and includes both a regular counter-subject and a redundant entry (flute, bars 17–19). The episode that follows introduces a new idea in thirds, which is to bear important fruit later on, and leads to a counter-exposition in which the *ripieno* instruments join. The stretto at bars 39–40 is a recurring feature in the coda to the first section (bars 64–78) and also in the middle section, which, unlike that of most da capo arias, begins (at bar 79) and ends (at bar 232) in the same key (B minor). This long middle section falls into three subsections, the first dominated by a flowing eight-bar theme played first by the flute and then in turn by violin, harpsichord (in F♯ minor) and *ripieno* violin and viola (A major, *cantabile*). In the second subsection, beginning at bar 155, the harpsichord reclaims its status as principal soloist by detaching itself from the other solo instruments, which join (sometimes in unison) with the rest of the ensemble in antiphonal exchanges, punctuating the keyboard's development of the episode idea (now in tenths rather than thirds) with references to the fugue subject. This merges into the final subsection, beginning about bar 193, in which the *ripieno* strings provide minimal support for some further working-out of the episode motif in three-part counterpoint above a continuo bass. The repeat of bars 1–78 is indicated by a 'da capo' direction in the autograph score.

Concerto No. 6 in B♭ major, BWV 1051

[Allegro] – Adagio ma non tanto – Allegro

This was for a long time regarded as the Cinderella among the Brandenburg Concertos, and even today it is the one least likely to be performed on its own. The absence of violins and the inclusion of bass viols make it a difficult work to include in concerts given by a normally constituted string orchestra, and it is only when it is played on the correct instruments, and with a single instrument to each part, that its intimate, undemonstrative textures make their effect. An ensemble of relatively low-pitched string instruments inevitably produces a somewhat subdued tone, and yet there is nothing essentially sombre about the music. Like Cinderella herself, the concerto does not flaunt its charms.

The claim that the sixth concerto is the earliest in the Brandenburg set was challenged in chapter 2 (see p. 14), but it must be conceded that the repeated quavers (viols, cello and continuo) of the opening ritornello place it very close to Vivaldi in style. Against the background of this mechanical iteration the two violas engage in close canon at the unison, the strictness of which is relaxed only occasionally and very briefly (at bars 8, 9–10, 12 and 16) when a change of harmony necessitates a small change of interval in the second part. This canon, incidentally, was the first thing in the Brandenburg Concertos to appear in print, when J. P. Kirnberger (who, it will be remembered, owned the autograph score) quoted the first four and a half bars of the two viola parts as an example of close canonic writing in his *Die Kunst des reinen Satzes in der Musik* (1771–9; vol. 2, part 2, pp. 57–8). It is no doubt the scoring of the opening ritornello that has led to the common misconception that the solo group in this concerto is formed by the two violas. Bach's own superscription, 'Concerto 6to à due

Viole da Braccio, due Viole da Gamba, Violoncello, Violone è Cembalo',
makes no distinction between solo and *ripieno* instruments, and in this it
recalls that of the third concerto. But this is not a concerto like
Brandenburg No. 3, in which each instrument or instrumental group is
allotted a solo role in turn. It becomes apparent as the first movement
unfolds, and even more apparent in the ritornello structure of the last
movement, that Bach treats the two violas and the cello as the solo group.
In other words he places the members of the new violin family in the
foreground, those of the older viol family in the background, almost as if
he intended an allegory on the changes taking place at the time in the
development of string instruments.

The structure of the first movement is summarized schematically in
Table 5. The opening ritornello is noteworthy not only for its combination of strict canon and what might be termed *Trommelbass* texture
(the 'drum bass' here applied to the middle parts as well), but also
because it shows nothing of the division into *Vordersatz*, *Fortspinnung* and
Epilog that we have observed in other ritornello movements. What Bach
does, in fact, is to transfer this tripartite division to the first episode (see
Ex. 19), thereby defining the three elements that make up the entire
material for all the subsequent episodes (motifs a, b and c in Table 5).
The separation of ritornello and episodes is by no means as rigid as might
be suggested by Table 5, however; canonic writing and *Trommelbass*
texture are sometimes present in the episodes as well as in the ritornellos,
and there is an obvious connexion between the ritornello theme and the
first of the episode motifs.

As in all the other Brandenburg Concertos except No. 4, Bach reduces
the forces required for the slow movement, in this case to the three
soloists (violas and cello) and continuo. The bass viols remain silent, and
the staves allotted to them are filled with rests. This led Martin Geck to
assert, in support of his conviction that the concerto is an arrangement of
an earlier work, that Bach had included staves for the viols because he
had not at that stage decided on the final scoring of the slow movement.[47]
Geck's statement that in the other concertos Bach was punctilious in
drawing exactly the number of staves required for the instrumentation of
each movement is, however, contradicted in the Adagio of the first
concerto, where the staves for the silent horns are likewise filled with
rests. That the slow movement of the sixth concerto has, nevertheless,
undergone some measure of revision or correction is suggested by the fact
that from bar 39 onwards the music has been copied on a sheet originally

Table 5 *Brandenburg Concerto No. 6: first movement*

Bar nos. (total)	Ritornello/episode	Keys	Remarks
1–17 (17)	Ritornello 1	B♭ maj	single motif (bars 1–5) repeated and extended in close canon
17–25 (9)	Episode 1	B♭–F maj	for motifs *a*, *b* and *c*, see Ex.19
25–8 (4)	Ritornello 2	F–B♭ maj	single statement of ritornello motif
29–46 (18)	Episode 2	B♭ maj–C min	motifs *a*, *b*, *c*, *a*
46–52 (7)	Ritornello 3	C min	two statements of ritornello motif
53–73 (21)	Episode 3	C–G min	further development of motifs *a*, *b*, *a*, *b*, *c*
73–80 (8)	Ritornello 4	G min	new extension of single motif
80–86 (7)	Episode 4	G min–E♭ maj	motif *a*
86–91 (6)	Ritornello 5	E♭ maj	two statements of ritornello motif
92–114 (23)	Episode 5		
92–102 (11)		E♭–B♭ maj	motifs *a*, *b*, *c*, *a*
103–14 (12)		B♭ maj	recapitulation of bars 17–25, modified to remain in B♭ and extended by varied repeat of last 4 bars
114–30 (17)	Ritornello 6	B♭ maj	exact repetition of Ritornello 1

Ex. 19   Brandenburg Concerto No. 6, first movement

intended for the last movement, and therefore ruled to accommodate seven bars to each system. The tell-tale erasure of every second bar-line, as originally drawn, is clearly visible.

This slow movement is the only one in the Brandenburgs to begin not in the relative minor of the concerto's main tonality, but in the subdominant major (E♭); the movement does, however, end in G minor. To begin and end a movement in different keys like this is unusual, but not unique: the Largo of Bach's Organ Sonata BWV 526 begins in E♭ and ends in C minor, and the Adagio of Corelli's Violin Sonata Op. 5 No. 5 has exactly the same tonal organization as the slow movement of Brandenburg No. 6. The music's fabric consists of the contrapuntal working-out of a single 'fugue' theme and its counter-subject over a continuo bass, cadencing in B♭ major (bar 11), E♭ major (20), F minor (30) and A♭ major (40); the bass then takes over the 'fugue' theme and, after two false starts, uses it to take the music into its 'proper' key of G minor, in which the violas play it, together with the counter-subject, for the last time. The expected cadence in G minor at bar 54 is side-stepped and postponed to bar 59, which gives the cello a chance to assert itself again as a member of the solo group with a quaver excursion against static chords.

The bass part that pursues its purposeful course through most of this movement has presented problems for both performers and commentators. It is shared, on two staves, by the cello and the violone (with harpsichord), the former in an unbroken crotchet line, the violone shadowing it in longer notes for the most part, with occasional passages in which the two string instruments are more independent of each other. Bars 27–36 illustrate both textures (Ex. 20). Laurence Dreyfus presents convincing evidence to show that the violone that Bach was writing for here was the six-string instrument with G' as its lowest note, sounding at the written pitch.[48] He points to a passage (bars 56–8) in the first movement which on a 16-foot instrument would produce an unlikely three-octave gap between the violone and the cello, and also to the low $B♭'$ at bars 45 and 110 of the third movement, which would have been unobtainable on any violone sounding an octave below the written pitch. As Dreyfus points out, however, in the slow movement a violone sounding at the written pitch interferes with the cello line even more than one sounding an octave lower, and to avoid this he suggests 'that the violone was *tacet* and that only the harpsichord continued to accompany, following the example of the slow movement to Concerto No. 2'. He goes on to say that 'in both instances Bach's score is unclear'. This is not the case, however. At the end of the first movement of Brandenburg no. 2 Bach clearly writes against the violone part the words 'Andante *tacet*' and against the cello and harpsichord part 'Andante sequit[ur]'. There is no similar tacet indication in the violone part of no. 6 in any of the surviving scores (including the autograph) or in the parts copied by Johann August Patzig (1738–1816), C. F. Zelter's assistant at the Singakademie in Berlin,[49] and it seems by no means unlikely that Bach did intend the heterophony that results from the combination of cello, violone and harpsichord. The 'interference' is, after all, not really injurious and it occurs elsewhere (bars 91–4 of the first movement; bars 29–31 of the last movement), admittedly at a faster tempo. Omission of the violone certainly makes for a clearer bass line in the slow movement;[50] on the other hand, there are several passages that benefit from the violone's participation, including bars 31–4 (see Ex. 20) and the octave statement of the 'fugue' theme at bars 44–7.

Ex. 20 Brandenburg Concerto No. 6, second movement

An elaborated Phrygian cadence leads into the last movement. This is perhaps the most tuneful of all Bach's concerto movements, and may, indeed, be regarded as a sprightly first cousin of the beguiling Sinfonia from the second part of the *Christmas Oratorio*, which opens with strikingly similar harmonies and melodic contour. The last movement of Brandenburg no. 6 is also structurally one of the least complicated concerto movements, and therefore demands little in the way of analytical comment here. The usual three limbs can be observed in the dance-like opening ritornello, but *Fortspinnung* is hardly the term for the syncopated continuation of the main motif, nor *Epilog* for the summary cadence at bar 8. Much of the material for the episodes in the first section is derived from the ritornello, easing the frequent and often fleeting transitions from one to the other – though the ritornellos remain easily identified by the merging into unison of the violas. The middle section (bars 46–65), which follows the standard course from relative to mediant minor (G minor–D minor), brings a new idea in lively discourse between the two violas, but there is also some recapitulation of episodic material from the first section and, once again, pertinent reminders of the ritornello motifs. The final section (bars 66–110) is a da capo repeat of the first.

This last movement serves as a welcome reminder that, for all the problems and uncertainties with which the Brandenburg Concertos confront the modern scholar and performer, Bach intended them for the enjoyment of his patrons and his fellow musicians. It would be difficult to imagine a more delightful and captivating conclusion to a set of *concerts avec plusieurs instruments*.

Notes

1 Background

1 See H. J. Marx, 'Einleitung', in *Arcangelo Corelli: historisch-critische Gesamtausgabe der musikalischen Werke*, vol. 5 (Cologne, 1976), pp. 22–3.

2 Both margraves were descended from the Elector Johann Georg of Brandenburg (1525–98), Christian Ludwig in the main line of descent from Johann Georg's first wife, Princess Sophie of Liegnitz, and Georg Friedrich from his third wife, Elisabeth of Anhalt, whose second son, Joachim Ernst (1583–1625), re-established the Ansbach dynasty. See *Mémoires pour servir à l'histoire de la maison de Brandebourg* [by King Frederick II of Prussia] (Berlin and The Hague, 1751), genealogical table.

3 The only vocal piece that Corelli is known to have written is a cantata, *Risonate amiche trombe (La fama)* for the annual festivities of the Accademia del Disegno di San Luca in Rome in 1702; the music is lost. See F. Piperno, 'Anfion in Campidoglio', in *Nuovissimi studi corelliani*, ed. S. Durante and P. Petrobelli (Florence, 1982), pp. 151–209.

4 *BD*, vol. 3, pp. 649–50.

5 See R. Bunge, 'Johann Sebastian Bachs Kapelle zu Cöthen und deren nachgelassene Instrumente', *Bach-Jahrbuch*, 2 (1905), pp. 14–47.

6 Christoph Wolff, on the other hand, has argued strongly against the traditional division of Bach's career into discrete chronological periods, each associated with a particular creative phase. He argues for a Leipzig origin for both the A minor solo concerto and the double concerto in his 'Bach's Leipzig chamber music', *Early Music*, 13 (1985), pp. 165–75, reprinted in C. Wolff, *Bach: Essays on his Life and Music* (Cambridge, Massachusetts, 1991), pp. 223–38.

7 P. Drummond, *The German Concerto*, p. 3.

8 K. Beckmann, 'Meck, Joseph', in *The New Grove Dictionary of Music and Musicians*, ed. S. Sadie (London, 1980), vol. 12, p. 10.

9 J. N. Forkel, *Über Johann Sebastian Bachs Leben, Kunst und Kunstwerke* (Leipzig, 1802; English translation, 1820), pp. 39–40.

10 Ibid., p. 112.

11 C. Wolff, *Bach: Essays on his Life and Music*, p. 75.

12 Vivaldi's influence on Bach's concerto style is explored in detail in H.-G. Klein, *Der Einfluß der vivaldischen Konzertform im Instrumentalwerk Johann Sebastian Bachs* (Strasbourg and Baden-Baden, 1970).

2 Genesis and reception

1 See *Bach-Jahrbuch*, 43 (1956), pp. 18–35.

2 J. G. Walther, *Musicalisches Lexicon, oder Musicalische Bibliothec* (Leipzig, 1732), p. 224.

3 R. Eitner, *Biographisch-bibliographisches Quellen-Lexikon der Musiker und Musikgelehrten der christlichen Zeitrechnung bis zur Mitte des neunzehnten Jahrhunderts*, vol. 2 (Leipzig,

1901), p. 418.

4 For a complete list of sources see the Kritische Bericht to *NBA*, vol. VII/ii. Most of the secondary sources date from the late eighteenth century.

5 In BWV 208 the flutes are required only once, in the well-known aria 'Schafe können sicher weiden', which does not include oboes. The oboists could therefore have doubled as flautists in this cantata.

6 J. Krey, 'Zur Entstehungsgeschichte des ersten Brandenburgischen Konzerts', pp. 339–40.

7 The score of the sinfonia actually specifies three oboes, but the range of the third oboe part (doubling viola) in the minuet clearly calls for a *taille*; in the First Brandenburg Concerto this part has been rewritten for the normal oboe, avoiding the low notes in the sinfonia.

8 H. Fitzpatrick, *The Horn and Horn-Playing* (London, 1970), pp. 20–21.

9 To draw attention to such a tenuous connexion may seem like special pleading, but similar thematic correspondences between a sinfonia and an opening recitative are frequently and unmistakably present in the cantatas, serenatas and even operas of Alessandro Scarlatti, and Bach may have been following a well-established tradition.

10 J. Tiersot, 'Sur les origines de la symphonie: une "sinfonia" de Jean-Sébastien Bach', in *Mélanges de musicologie offerts à M. Lionel de la Laurencie* (Paris, 1933), pp. 177–84; R. Gerber, *Bachs Brandenburgische Konzerte*, p. 57.

11 Michael Marissen, in particular, has advanced strong arguments for questioning the linking of the Sinfonia with BWV 208; see his 'Scoring, Structure, and Signification', pp. 46–67.

12 H. Besseler, 'Zur Chronologie der Konzerte'; see also the same author's Kritische Bericht to *NBA*, vol. VII/ii, pp. 23–8, and his introduction to the study score based on the *NBA* (Kassel and Leipzig, 1957), with English translation by H. F. Redlich.

13 Besseler's chronology for the instrumental works usually assigned to the Cöthen years has been expertly challenged by Hans-Joachim Schulze. See Schulze's 'Johann Sebastian Bachs Konzerte: Fragen der Überlieferung und Chronologie'.

14 In *The New Grove Bach Family* (London, 1983), a separate reprint of the *New Grove* article, this was changed to 'by 24 March 1721', about which there can be no doubt at all.

15 See the notes accompanying the 1971 recording of the Brandenburg Concertos by the Academy of St Martin in the Fields, conducted by Sir Neville Marriner, on Philips, 426 088–2.

16 M. Geck, 'Gattungstraditionen und Altersschichten'.

17 M. Bernstein, 'The chronology of the orchestral suites, BWV 1066–1069', in *Report of the Eighth Congress of the International Musicological Society, New York 1961* (Kassel, 1962), vol. 2, pp. 127–8.

18 S. Germann, 'The Mietkes, the Margrave and Bach', p. 128.

19 Ibid., n.37. The upper range of both instruments was later extended to e'''.

20 Both the Mietke instruments at the Charlottenburg extended down to F. See S. Germann, 'The Mietkes, the Margrave and Bach', pp. 146–7.

21 Christopher Hogwood, in the notes to his recording of the work (L'Oiseau-Lyre, 414 187), points out that a literal interpretation of bars 192–3 in the cadenza would require a pedal harpsichord, since the player's left hand must otherwise stretch an eleventh above the A pedal point in the bass. It is not impossible, though, that here (as occasionally elsewhere in his keyboard music) Bach intended notational consistency to take precedence over practical considerations.

22 P. Williams, 'Bach's G minor Sonata for viola da gamba and harpsichord: a seventh Brandenburg Concerto?', *Early Music*, 12 (1984), pp. 345–54.

23 Persuasive arguments are presented by Walter F. Hindermann (*Widergewonnene*

Schwesterwerke der Brandenburgischen Konzerte Johann Sebastian Bachs (Hofheim am Taunus, 1972), pp. 25–40) to show that the opening sinfonia and first aria of Cantata No. 42 originated as movements from a lost concerto for two oboes, bassoon, strings and continuo. Hindermann's identification of the aria 'Lasset dem Höchsten ein Danklied erschallen' from Cantata No. 66 as the last movement of the same concerto is less convincing, as also is his claim to have found another 'sister' for the Brandenburgs in three movements from Cantatas Nos. 99, 125 and 115 (ibid., pp. 43–71).

24 P. Spitta, *Johann Sebastian Bach* (Leipzig, 1873–80; English translation by Clara Bell and J. G. Fuller-Maitland, 1884–5), vol. 2, p. 129.

25 G. Schünemann, 'Die Bachpflege der Berliner Singakademie', *Bach-Jahrbuch*, 25 (1928), pp. 138–71.

26 Both letters are quoted in K. Heller, 'Die Konzerte in der Bachpflege', p. 134; the punctuation has been modified in these translations. The 'concerto for piano with 2 oblig. flutes a bec' is, of course, Bach's keyboard arrangement (BWV 1057) of the Fourth Brandenburg Concerto. It is somewhat surprising that Dehn refers to it in this context (it was, after all, known to both Forkel and Bach's sons), but the autograph was in the same Berlin library as the Brandenburg Concertos and would have come under Dehn's scrutiny at this time.

27 See note 15, above. Dart died on 6 March 1971, before the recording sessions were complete. He played the harpsichord continuo in the third concerto and the first movements of the second and fourth concertos.

28 L. Dreyfus, *Bach's Continuo Group*, pp. 142–51.

3 Instrumentation

1 This was not, however, the case in England, where the favourite title for works in a Corellian disposition was 'Concerto's in seven parts'; but the English often used also 'Grand Concertos' (a literal translation of 'Concerti grossi') for both new works of this type and reissues of *concerti grossi* by foreign composers. Handel's op. 6 set (1740) were announced as 'Twelve Grand Concerto's in Seven Parts'.

2 A. Hutchings, 'Concerto: 2. Origins to 1750', in *The New Grove Dictionary of Music and Musicians*, ed. S. Sadie (London, 1980), vol. 4, p.631. In the opinion of Michael Marissen ('Scoring, Structure, and Signification', pp. 221–2) concertos nos. 1 and 6 are ensemble concertos, nos. 2 and 5 are *concerti grossi* and nos. 3 and 4 'juxtapose the two styles at the center of the collection'.

3 Hutchings, 'Concerto', p. 628.

4 This seems to have been the implication, too, behind Joseph Maximilian III's title, *Concerti ... a più istromenti cioè violini, corni da caccia, viole, trombe, bassi, flauti traversi, oboe* (Verona, 1765).

5 Leopold Mozart referred to the violino piccolo as a concerto instrument (see note 16, below), but no concertos for it, apart from Brandenburg no. 1, seem to have survived.

6 T. Dart, 'Bach's "fiauti d'echo"'.

7 It is not at all surprising, in a work in G major, that the first *fiauto* never, and the second seldom, descends below *g'*.

8 N. Carrell, *Bach's Brandenburg Concertos*, pp. 85–6.

9 The *f♯'''* is sometimes found in a weak context (as in bar 51 etc.), but only once in the concerto does Bach place it on a strong beat – in the last movement at bar 57; as Michael Marissen points out ('Scoring, Structure, and Signification', p. 86), the only way to produce the note perfectly in tune is to finger a *g'''* with the instrument's end-hole closed against the player's leg, a technique which is quite practicable here. Marissen comes down strongly in support of the treble recorder in F as the instrument required for the *fiauti d'echo* parts in Brandenburg Concerto No. 4.

10   D. Lasocki, 'Paisible's echo flute'; F. Morgan, J. Martin and M. Tattersall, 'Echoes resounding', *The Recorder: Journal of the Victorian Recorder Guild*, 10 (December 1989), pp. 19–24.

11   See *Mémoires pour servir à l'histoire de la maison de Brandebourg*, genealogical table.

12   The *NBA* edition of both the First Brandenburg Concerto and the Sinfonia BWV 1046*a* not only specifies 'Fagotto' for what Bach calls 'Bassono', but does so in a way which misleadingly suggests that 'Fagotto' is found in the sources.

13   A similar example in N. Carrell, *Bach's Brandenburg Concertos*, p. 35, fails to include the B♮'s in the first horn part at bar 56 of the first movement and in the second horn part at bar 33.

14   Ibid., p. 62.

15   E. H. Tarr, 'Trumpet', *The New Grove Dictionary of Musical Instruments*, ed. S. Sadie (London, 1984), vol. 3, p. 651.

16   L. Mozart, *Versuch einer gründlicher Violinschule* (Augsburg, 1756; English translation by E. Knocker, 1948), p. 10.

17   Observing this, Michael Marissen ('Scoring, Structure, and Signification', p. 162) suggests that Bach may have conceived the parts for a smaller tenor viol with its lowest string tuned to G; the two tenor viols would then balance the two violas (or tenor violins) in the other group. Thurston Dart had earlier made a similar suggestion (see the notes to his 1971 recording on Philips 426 088–2).

18   L. Dreyfus, *Bach's Continuo Group*, pp. 142–51.

19   See especially J. W. Finson, 'The Violone in Bach's Brandenburg Concerti', *The Galpin Society Journal*, 29 (1976), pp. 104–11.

20   To mention just one example, observe how the violone part at the opening of the Fifth Brandenburg Concerto doubles the cello and cembalo parts except in the one passage (bar 4) where the line obviously dips below the instrument's lowest note (*D*). Cf. also bars 124, 138 and 222 in the same movement.

21   D. Speer, *Grund-richter ... Unterricht der musicalischen Kunst, oder Vierfaches musicalisches Kleeblatt* (Ulm, 1697), pp. 206–7.

22   'Das große Clavecin oder flügel mit 2 Clavituren, von Michael Mietke in Berlin, 1719: defect' (Hist. Staatsarchiv Oranienbaum, Abt. Köthen, St. A. a2. Nr. 32, fol. 12v); see *BD*, vol. 2, p. 74.

23   See S. Germann, 'The Mietkes, the Margrave and Bach'.

24   Bach's intentions in this regard were not fully realized. See p. 89.

4 The dedication score and its design

1   Georg von Dadelsen was the first to point out that a second hand has shared the copying of the polonaise and the trio for horns and oboes on the last page (fol. 14r) of the first concerto. See G. von Dadelsen, *Beiträge zur Chronologie der Werke Johann Sebastian Bachs*, Tübinger Bach-Studien, Heft 4/5 (Trossingen, 1958), p. 84.

2   For examples of both corrected and uncorrected errors in Bach's manuscript, see P. Wackernagel, 'Beobachtungen am Autograph von Bachs Brandenburgischen Konzerten'.

3   In the cadenza of the fifth concerto; see below, p. 89.

4   C. Wolff, 'Die Rastrierungen in den Originalhandschriften Joh. Seb. Bachs und ihre Bedeutung für die diplomatische Quellenkritik', in *Festschrift für Friedrich Smend zum 70. Geburtstag* (Berlin, 1963), pp. 80–92.

5 The ritornello structure

1   P. Spitta, *Johann Sebastian Bach*, vol. 1, p. 407; Eng. trans., vol. 1, pp. 408–9.

2   Ibid., vol. 1, pp. 735–43; Eng. trans., vol. 2, pp. 129–36.

3 A. Halm, 'Über J. S. Bachs Konzertform'; W. Krüger, 'Das Concerto grosso Joh. Seb. Bachs', *Bach-Jahrbuch*, 29 (1932), pp. 1–50.

4 R. Gerber, *Bachs Brandenburgische Konzerte*.

5 V. Protopopov, 'Das Da-capo-Prinzip in den Konzerten Johann Sebastian Bachs', in *Beiträge zum Konzertschaffen Johann Sebastian Bachs* (Bach-Studien 6), ed. P. Ahnsehl, K. Heller and H.-J. Schulze (Leipzig, 1981).

6 See especially his essay 'The Classical concerto', in *Essays in Musical Analysis*, vol. 3 (1936), pp. 3–27.

7 J. A. Fuller-Maitland, *Bach's 'Brandenburg' Concertos* (the quoted passage is on p. 40); N. Carrell, *Bach's Brandenburg Concertos*.

8 M. Bukofzer, *Music in the Baroque Era* (New York, 1947; see especially pp. 227–8); A. J. B. Hutchings, *A Companion to Mozart's Piano Concertos* (London, 1948), and *The Baroque Concerto* (1959).

9 M. Talbot, *Vivaldi* (London, 1978), p. 144.

10 The key schemes shown here are those most frequently to be found in da capo arias by Alessandro Scarlatti and his contemporaries. Modifications are not unusual, not least in Bach's arias.

11 See R. L. Marshall, *The Compositional Process of J. S. Bach*, vol. 1 (Princeton, 1972), pp. 36–7 and 119–30.

12 On Bach's so-called free da capo arias, see especially S. A. Crist, 'Aria Forms in the Vocal Works of J. S. Bach, 1714–1724,' (PhD dissertation, Brandeis University, 1988); and M. K. Whaples, 'Bach's earliest arias', *Bach: the Journal of the Riemenschneider Bach Institute*, 20/1 (Spring 1989), pp. 31–54. See also M. Boyd, *Bach* (London, 1983), pp. 131–3.

13 Among dozens of other examples may be mentioned the well-known 'Erbarme dich' from the *St Matthew Passion*. The bass aria 'Komm, süßes Kreuz' from the same work is one of about ten examples which employ a subdominant 'recapitulation', anticipating a procedure found in some sonata-form movements by Mozart and Schubert.

14 See, for example, the aria 'Das Blut, so meine Schuld durchstricht' from Cantata No. 78, *Jesu, der du meine Seele*. Presumably the influence here is from the concerto to the aria, rather than the other way about.

15 W. Fischer, 'Zur Entwicklungsgeschichte des Wiener klassischen Stils', *Studien zur Musikwissenschaft*, 3 (1915), pp. 24–84.

16 Michael Marissen ('Scoring, Structure, and Signification', p. 226) argues that this ritornello employs only the two outer segments of the *Fortspinnungstypus*, bars 1–3 forming the 'forepiece' (*Vordersatz*) and the rest an 'epilogue' (*Epilog*) which divides into two subsections at bar 6. Obviously one cannot afford to be dogmatic in dissecting what the composer probably thought of as a single 'statement' anyway.

17 M. Talbot, *Vivaldi*, p. 143. Here only the first four bars of the eighteen-bar episode return; the material that effected the modulation from tonic to dominant in the first episode is entirely replaced.

18 The term 'da capo' is preferred to the more general 'ternary' for such movements as this, since the implications it carries about the tonal and melodic (ritornello) structure are here fulfilled. In the sources (including the autograph) the repeat of the first section is not written out, but simply indicated by the direction 'Da capo'. For a blueprint of da capo form, see page 47.

6 The individual concertos

1 Spitta certainly regarded the Minuet as an appendage to the first three movements of the concerto, and as 'a concession to the taste of the time'; he suggested that it might be omitted in performance. See P. Spitta, *Johann Sebastian Bach* (Eng. trans.), vol. 1, p. 132.

2 The evidence for this derives largely from details in the autograph score of BWV 1046. For example, the nature of certain transcription errors in the violino piccolo part, both corrected (I, bars 22 and 30; II, bar 17) and uncorrected (I, bar 8; II, bar 27), strongly suggest that this was copied from a version for normal violin notated a minor third higher. As will be shown later, there are also some details in Penzel's score which probably did not originate with Bach.

3 P. Spitta, *Johann Sebastian Bach* (Eng. trans.), vol. 2, p. 627.

4 A. Dürr, *Die Kantaten von Johann Sebastian Bach* (Kassel, 1971; 4th edn, 1981), pp. 681–2: '... dieser Umformungsprozeß ist eine bewundernswerte Leistung Bachs ... In der ... Bruchlosigkeit, mit der sich der Chorsatz dem Instrumentalpart einfügt, als habe er ihm schon von allem Anfang an zugehört, offenbart sich die reife Meisterschaft, die der einundvierzigjährige Bach erlangt hatte.'

5 G. Butler, 'J. S. Bach and the concord–discord paradox', p. 352. Puzzling is Butler's statement that 'in the concerto, the concertino is made up of three parts, for violino I, II and viola respectively'.

6 Ibid., p. 350.

7 The single instance of quadruple stopping at bar 25 would be impossible to play on an ordinary violin (as would several other passages in the movement). The notes of the chords could, of course, have been redistributed in such a way as to employ the lowest string, but not without sacrificing the part-writing implicit in the passage as a whole.

8 For example, the opening choruses of Cantatas Nos. 11, *Lobet Gott in seinen Reichen* (Ascension Oratorio, 1735); 70a, *Wachet, betet, seid bereit allezeit* (1716); and 193, *Ihr Tore zu Zion* (c.1727).

9 S. A. Crist, 'Aria Forms in the Vocal Works of J. S. Bach, 1714–1724', pp. 150–51. Crist is here describing arias of the period 1714–24, but his observation holds good also for choruses not based on a chorale melody.

10 J. Butt, *Bach: Mass in B minor* (Cambridge, 1991), p. 71.

11 The *first* movement of the Concerto for Three Harpsichords in D minor, BWV 1063, uses the rhythm in question, but its minor tonality and stepwise movement are untypical of the type of expression under consideration here.

12 Berlin, Staatsbibliothek Preußischer Kulturbesitz, Mus. ms. Bach, P 174.

13 W. Neumann, Kritische Bericht to *NBA*, vol. I/38, p. 51.

14 The phrase 'vereinigte Zwietracht' almost defies translation in this context, uniting as it does the concept of *concordia discors* ('discordant concord'), or the juxtaposition of opposites, with the idea of litigation successfully resolved. See G. Butler, especially pp. 344–50.

15 Klaus Häfner (*Aspekte des Parodieverfahrens bei Johann Sebastian Bach* (Laaber, 1987), p. 180) quotes an aria from a Council Election cantata text by Picander (BWV Anh. 3) to support his view that the versification of BWV 207/1 is not so very unusual, but this seems a trifle disingenuous; compared with the generality of cantata verse, *Vereinigte Zwietracht* is quite definitely something of an anomaly.

16 In da capo strophes where the A section consists of two lines of verse, it is usual for the second line to rhyme with the last word of the B section. A rhyme between the first line of A and the last of B is also quite common but, except where the two lines of A rhyme with each other, it is unusual (though not unknown) for there to be no rhyme at all between the A and B sections. In the case of *Vereinigte Zwietracht* the poet perhaps intended the first three lines, and not the first two, to form the A section; this would have completed the sense and syntax of that section, as well as providing a rhyme with the end of the B section.

17 F. Smend, *Bach in Köthen* (Berlin, 1951; English translation by John Page, ed. S. Daw, St Louis, 1985), p. 34 and *passim*. Very little of this music survives in its original form.

18 Michael Marissen ('Scoring, Structure, and Signification', pp. 33–4) rightly takes me to

task for having suggested (in *Bach*, p. 81) that the cantata chorus may have originated in an earlier vocal composition *in D major*. The key of the supposed original, however, has no bearing on the theory that Bach chose a violino piccolo because of its ability to deal effectively with chords in an F major piece. Marissen acknowledges that even in this movement (let alone the others) the violino piccolo fails to establish itself as a genuine concerto soloist. He equates the instrument with the person of a courtly *Konzertmeister* and suggests that the composer, as *Kapellmeister*, is here deliberately taking him down a peg or two. In a similar way, the 'raising up' of the lowly recorders and the 'bringing down' of the principal violin in the Fourth Brandenburg Concerto are presented as an allegory of 'the breach between appearance and essence familiar from everyday social and religious experience' (p. 117). Marissen again seems to credit Bach with Marxist intentions when he suggests that Prince Leopold would have been struck by the social implications of the sixth concerto, in which 'humble orchestral ripieno instruments [the violas] play brilliant, solo chamber musicians' parts and privileged solo chamber instruments [the bass viols] (perhaps favorites of Prince Leopold himself) play routine, ripieno musicians' parts' (p. 166).

19 The suspicion might arise that it was Penzel also who altered the harmony on the fourth quaver of bar 1 and in similar contexts in the first movement in order to avoid the simultaneous sounding of a tonic triad in the oboes and a dominant triad in the strings. This is, however, contradicted by mistranscriptions of the second violin part in the autograph (f' instead of e' in bar 27; e' altered to d' in bar 43), which strongly suggest that the 6-4 harmony of the earlier version was Bach's own.

20 The term is derived from the distinctive cadence formed in the Phrygian mode, the only one of the old church modes in which the second note is a semitone above the final (E). In sixteenth-century polyphony C was preferred to B for intermediate cadences in the Phrygian mode, since Renaissance theory and notation did not admit the note D♯ needed to form the third of a major triad on B. This explains the importance that Baroque composers attached to mediant minor tonality as a structural pillar in major-key pieces (the mediant minor is the key normally found at the end of the B section in major-key da capo arias, for instance; see the diagram on p. 47), and this I–iii relationship persisted into the nineteenth century (in the first movement of Brahms's Second Piano Concerto, for example).

21 One cannot help regretting that, in securing a better distribution of the last two chords than he had achieved in the sinfonia, Bach felt obliged to introduce quaver movement into the second violin part (changing the German sixth into a French sixth) in order to avoid consecutive fifths with the bass.

22 French Suite No. 6, BWV 817; Orchestral Suite No. 2, BWV 1067.

23 See J. Eppelsheim, 'The Instruments', in *Johann Sebastian Bach: Life, Times, Influence*, ed. B. Schwendowius and W. Dömling (Hamburg, 1977), p. 135.

24 See, for example, bars 2–6.

25 More problematic is the reading of bar 37, where the first $e♮$ in the continuo and bassoon parts of BWV 52 seems to solve the ambiguity of the earlier sources, both of which lack an accidental here (Besseler in the *NBA* prefers an $e♭$ in both the Brandenburg and the Sinfonia versions; Rust in the *BG* edition of the concerto chose $e♮$, while Alfred Dörffel, who edited the sinfonia for the *BG*, preferred $e♭$). However, the corresponding $a♮$ in bar 66 of BWV 52 is met by an unequivocal $a♭$ in the autograph of the Brandenburg version.

26 A. Basso, *Frau Musika*, vol. 1, p. 582.

27 E. Lang-Becker, *Bach: die Brandenburgischen Konzerte*, pp. 40–44.

28 As mentioned elsewhere (see p. 33), this is one of the very few passages, outside the fifth concerto, in which the bass is figured in the dedication score. Lang-Becker (p. 43) suggests that Bach made the chromatic alteration in bar 112 to spell out his name in the bass of bars 109–112 (in German, B = B♭ and H = B♮). The unusually precise and

carefully notated dynamic shadings in this passage, incidentally, are a feature of the movement as a whole.

29 M. Geck, 'Gattungstraditionen und Altersschichten', pp. 141–5.

30 A. Mendel, Kritischer Bericht to *NBA*, vol. I/xiv (Kassel, 1963), pp. 106–7.

31 H.-J. Schulze, 'Johann Sebastian Bachs Konzerte', pp. 18–19.

32 Score and parts are in the Staatsbibliothek Preußischer Kulturbesitz, Berlin (P 1063 and St 638 respectively).

33 N. Carrell, *Bach's Brandenburg Concertos*, p. 78.

34 E. Platen, 'Zum Problem des Mittelsatzes im dritten Brandenburgischen Konzert Bachs', p. 62. In this case, however, Bach's 'borrowings' extend to all three movements, the first and last deriving from the prelude and fugue in A minor, BWV 894.

35 Ibid., pp. 67–70. Curiously, Platen chose not to retain Bach's distribution of the notes in the two cadential chords that form the frame for his 'improvisation'.

36 In considering the changes to the cello and continuo parts it should be borne in mind that these were possibly copied from an earlier version of the movement, and that such passages as bars 9–10 in the Brandenburg version might incorporate later improvements.

37 It is perhaps not until the first movement of Mendelssohn's E minor Violin Concerto (1844) that we find a solo violin again performing this function in a concerto (first movement, bars 131–9 and 377–85).

38 Alfred Dürr lists no fewer than twenty sources (twelve scores and eight sets of parts) in the Kritische Bericht to his edition of BWV 1050a (see n. 40). These include some nineteenth-century copies.

39 The scribe in question was until recently thought to be Bach's successor in Leipzig, Gottlob Harrer.

40 The early version of the Fifth Brandenburg Concerto (given the BWV number 1050a) was published in 1975 as an appendix to the *NBA*, edited by Alfred Dürr; it has been recorded by the Academy of Ancient Music directed by Christopher Hogwood (L'Oiseau-Lyre, 414 187).

41 D. Forman, *Mozart's Concerto Form: the First Movements of the Piano Concertos* (London, 1971).

42 Note how Bach changes the second note in the flute part from a'' at bar 49 to g'' at bar 145 (tenth note) to avoid consecutive fifths with the altered left hand of the harpsichord.

43 In its early version this solo passage is akin to that in bars 146–72 of the D minor Harpsichord Concerto, BWV 1052 (first movement), which performs a similar function with minimal string support.

44 C. Wolff, 'Die Rastrierungen in den Originalhandschriften Joh. Seb. Bachs', pp. 80–92. Wolff accounts for the presence of the longer cadenza in the autograph parts (St 130) by observing that both these and the dedication score must have been copied from a lost full score at about the same time.

45 J. J. Quantz, *Versuch einer Anweisung die Flöte traversiere zu spielen* (Berlin, 1752; 3rd edn, 1789; English translation by Edward R. Reilly, 1966), pp. 179–80.

46 R. L. Marshall, 'Tempo and dynamic indications in the Bach sources: a review of the terminology', in *Bach, Handel, Scarlatti: Tercentenary Essays*, ed. P. Williams (Cambridge, 1985), pp. 273–4.

47 M. Geck, 'Gattungstraditionen und Altersschichten', p. 148.

48 L. Dreyfus, *Bach's Continuo Group*, p. 150.

49 Berlin, Staatsbibliothek Preußischer Kulturbesitz, St. 150.

50 As in the recording by the Academy of Ancient Music, directed by Christopher Hogwood (see note 40 above).

Select bibliography

Basso, Alberto. *Frau Musika: la vita e le opere di J. S. Bach* (Turin, 1979–83), especially vol. 1, pp. 567–92

Besseler, Heinrich. 'Zur Chronologie der Konzerte Johann Sebastian Bachs', in *Festschrift Max Schneider zum achtzigsten Geburtstag*, ed. W. Vetter (Leipzig, 1955), pp. 115–28

'Markgraf Christian Ludwig von Brandenburg', *Bach-Jahrbuch*, 43 (1956), pp. 18–35

'Bemerkungen, J. S. Bachs Brandenburgische Konzerte betreffend', *Die Musikforschung*, 13 (1960), pp. 383–4

Butler, Gregory G. 'J. S. Bach and the concord–discord paradox', *The Journal of Musicology*, 9 (1991), pp. 343–57

Carrell, Norman, *Bach's Brandenburg Concertos* (London, 1963; reprinted 1985)

Dart, Thurston. 'Bach's "Fiauti d'Echo"', *Music and Letters*, 41 (1960), pp. 331–41

Dreyfus, Laurence. *Bach's Continuo Group: Players and Practices in His Vocal Works* (Cambridge, Massachusetts, 1987)

Drummond, Pippa. *The German Concerto: Five Eighteenth-Century Studies* (Oxford, 1980)

Dürr, Alfred. 'Zur Entstehungsgeschichte des 5. Brandenburgischen Konzerts', *Bach-Jahrbuch*, 41 (1975), pp. 63–9

Fuller-Maitland, J. A. *Bach's 'Brandenburg' Concertos* (London, 1929)

Geck, Martin. 'Gattungstradition und Altersschichten in den Brandenburgischen Konzerten', *Die Musikforschung*, 23 (1970), pp. 139–52

Gerber, Rudolf. *Bachs Brandenburgische Konzerte: eine Einführung in ihre formale und geistige Wesenart* (Kassel, 1951; 2nd edn 1965)

Germann, Sheridan. 'The Mietkes, the Margrave and Bach', in *Bach, Handel, Scarlatti: Tercentenary Essays*, ed. P. Williams (Cambridge, 1985), pp. 119–48

Günther, Ulrich. 'Das Instrumentarium in den "Brandenburgischen Konzerten" von J. S. Bach', *Musik im Unterricht*, 59 (1968), pp. 128–36

Halm, August. 'Über J. S. Bachs Konzertform', *Bach-Jahrbuch*, 16 (1919), pp. 1–44

Heller, Karl. 'Die Konzerte in der Bachpflege und im Bachbild des 18. und frühen 19. Jahrhunderts', in *Beiträge zum Konzertschaffen Johann Sebastian Bachs* (Bach-Studien 6, 1981), pp. 127–38

Hofmann, Richard. 'Die F-Trompete im 2. Brandenburgischen Konzert von Joh. Seb. Bach', *Bach-Jahrbuch*, 13 (1916), pp. 1–7

Hutchings, Arthur. *The Baroque Concerto* (London, 1959; 3rd edn, 1973)

Krey, Johannes. 'Zur Entstehungsgeschichte des ersten Brandenburgischen Konzerts', in *Festschrift Heinrich Besseler zum 60. Geburtstag* (Leipzig, 1961), pp. 337–42

Lang-Becker, Elke. *Bach: die Brandenburgischen Konzerte* (Munich, 1990)

Lenzewski, G. *Die Hohenzollern in der Musikgeschichte des 18. Jahrhunderts* (Berlin, 1926)

Lasocki, David. 'Paisible's Echo Flute, Bononcini's *Flauti Eco*, and Bach's *Fiauti d'Echo*', *The Galpin Society Journal*, 45 (1992), pp. 59–66

Marissen, Michael Anthony. 'Scoring, Structure, and Signification in J. S. Bach's Brandenburg Concertos' (PhD dissertation, Brandeis University, 1991)

Platen, Emil. 'Zum Problem des Mittelsatzes im dritten Brandenburgischen Konzert Bachs', in *Chorerziehung und neue Musik: für Kurt Thomas zum 65. Geburtstag*, ed. M. Kluge (Wiesbaden, 1969), pp. 58–70

Rienäcker, Gerd. 'Beobachtungen zur Dramaturgie im ersten Satz des 5. Brandenburgischen Konzerts', in *Beiträge zum Konzertschaffen Johann Sebastian Bachs* (Bach-Studien 6, 1981), pp. 63–79

Schulze, Hans-Joachim. 'Johann Sebastian Bachs Konzerte: Fragen der Übelieferung und Chronologie', in *Beiträge zum Konzertschaffen Johann Sebastian Bachs* (Bach-Studien 6, 1981), pp. 9–26

Steglich, Rudolf. 'Johann Sebastian Bachs drittes Brandenburgisches Konzert', in *Vom Nützlichen durchs Wahre zum Schönen: Festschrift für E. Madsack zum 75. Geburtstag* (Hanover, 1964), pp. 53–6

Wackernagel, Peter. 'Beobachtungen am Autograph von Bachs Brandenburgischen Konzerten', in *Festschrift Max Schneider zum achtzigsten Geburtstag*, ed. W. Vetter (Leipzig, 1955), pp. 129–38

Index

Index

Index